The Undesirable

AF725345

Sheza Jilal

chipmunkapublishing
the mental health publisher

Published by
Chipmunkapublishing
PO Box 6872
Brentwood
Essex CM13 1ZT
United Kingdom

http://www.chipmunkapublishing.com

Cover Artwork - Melbourne-based street artist 'Meek'

Chipmunkapublishing gratefully acknowledge the support of Arts Council England.

1. The fox and grapes
2. The girl with the dark eyes
3. Submission
4. Sanity check
5. The death of Eros
6. Lyon: city of light
7. The society for cutting up men
8. La maison des dingues
9. Apathy in the UK
10. Maria
11. Drunk in Johannesburg
12. Getting ‘one under’
13. Burning the bridges…
14. …the final bridge
15. Neither victim nor criminal

Chapter 1 – The fox and grapes

A flame-haired girl sat across the table from me with her back pressed against the wall. It had been a stifling afternoon, but it was getting much cooler now by the way the breeze from the open window stirred the blood-red flag hanging near it. She leant towards me resting her elbows on the table. Peering over the candles her long tresses fell forward half covering her face, the soft light illuminating her big blue eyes. I looked up at the creased, crimson cloth, looked to my sides and suddenly felt embarrassed. I had not even noticed that the flat was in such a state until she had too. Meaningless graffiti was scrawled across the walls of the flat and scattered around were the day's newspapers. All had the image of two large buildings with balls of fire erupting from them with a thick, black cloud spilling out of one and drifting upwards into the clear blue sky.

My kitchen was empty save a bottle of vinegar that had been there since I first moved in. Vinegar comes from the French word *vinaigre* – sour wine.

I looked straight into the girl's eyes, wishing I could say something to break the uncomfortable silence. I could have mentioned yesterday's carnage but I had nothing to say. I was then about to comment on the lines of thin scabs crisscrossing her arms but decided against. I didn't know if it would be right to talk about it or not.

'Candle light,' she then sighed, 'how romantic.'

'Yeah, well, the electricity meter has run out,' I said, 'so I'm going to have to charge the key tomorrow morning.'

'But the key contains emergency credit that you can use if...'

'That's what I've just used up.'

She rolled her eyes and shook her head, tossing her red mane.

'Shez, look at this place: are you really twenty?'

'So,' I butted in, 'I'm really sorry if everything isn't quite up to your standard at the moment.'

'Look, do you want me to go?' she asked.

'No, no!' I replied. 'Sorry, I've had a hard day...I mean...well.'

I did not want her to leave.

I swiftly lowered my gaze: a command that had been repeatedly drilled into me at mosque. For a moment I forgot that I was in the company of a woman and concentrated on what was in front of me. It was a small white paper with tobacco spread neatly across it. I picked up the little dark brown lump next to it and at the same time lit another half-melted candle that it was next to. She observed me burning the modest lump and sprinkling the residue over the tobacco.

'Low-grade Moroccan shit,' she remarked.

'What, me or the hash?' I asked.

She replied that she was sorry she did not know I was a Moroccan and that she thought I was Asian. I shrugged my shoulders, told her that people make that mistake all the time and carried on with what I was doing.

The flat had not always looked like this. The state provided me with it after I left my father and step-mother as a seventeen year old. At one time my new home was my castle until I started to whore this East End flat out to classmates at college who still lived with their parents. I'd lost count of the amount of people who'd had sex on my bed. Of the ones I remember there was Hannah, the sleepy-eyed brunette, who did it with Jonathan, the black leftie with dreadlocks. There was Jin-Jin, the slim Chinese with the red highlights, who did it with Adam, the tall Englishman who did not like Jonathan because he was black. There was this smart Bengali fashion victim who would give me £20 to borrow my spare key for the afternoon so he could do it with 'some blonde'. The money I made from this multicultural love fest I always spent on beer and hashish. I came home one evening to find a carrier bag on my table. I put my hand straight in and found myself clutching a pair of condoms with a whitish liquid oozing down my fingers. Soon afterwards I changed the locks and I barricaded myself inside and never let anyone else in. By the time I reached nineteen no one had any use for the flat anymore since they had all moved away from their parents too. It was around that moment that I started to graffiti the walls and destroy the furniture.

I opened a can of lager, looked up and noticed the girl again.

I observed her trying to pick something off the floor and place it on the table. I barely knew her and already she was taking over my flat. Suddenly I had gone from wanting to love this girl to loathing her. I no longer felt uneasy that I had forgotten her name. I decided to do a U-turn, just be myself and let her find out.

'Shez, you really need to sort this mess out!' she shrieked in a silly voice.

'Je vais l'faire demain mais laisse moi tranquille pour le moment!' I replied, making my way towards the bathroom.

I looked behind me to see the confusion in her face. I doubted she would be willing to enjoy the pleasure of my company for much longer.

'C'est mon appartement! C'est ma bière! Je suis un adulte! Maintenant laisse moi tranquille!'

I entered the pitch-black, windowless bathroom and slammed the door behind me. I silently stood there in the darkness and swiftly heard the sound of a door swinging open and then being slammed shut at the other end of the flat.

In one of Aesop's fables a fox is struggling to reach a bunch of mouth-watering grapes that are hanging from a vine high above his head. Eventually the fox gives up, reassuring himself that the grapes were probably sour anyway.

By means of a lighter from my back pocket I managed to find the toilet, aim correctly, flush, wash my hands and find the door to get out. I wiped my hands on the red flag since I could not find a towel, and promptly sat down. I suddenly noticed both a P45 form and a psychiatrist's report that were on the table and carelessly doodled all over them in green felt-tip pen.

Some time ago I had briefly made up with my family and was invited to come with them to Casablanca for a month. I had given the spare key to Jonathan so he could keep an eye on the place. Since I was yet to turn the flat into a brothel I warned him against any sexual liaisons taking place. He mentioned something about having to try not to. I asked him why he would have to try. He replied that accidents happen. I said that accidents do not happen but he insisted that they did. I asked him to explain bit by bit and he accused me of being 'difficult' and told me to 'grow up'.

I looked up at the rest of the table and realised that the girl had taken my entire lump of hash with her leaving me with a half empty can of warm beer. Sour grapes.

Chapter 2 – The girl with the dark eyes

A few weeks had passed. The fridge was still empty and a holy book had been defaced beyond recognition. The scattered remains of a wooden chair had to be thrown away, but next to the communal bins someone had dumped two white patio chairs, so I took them back to my flat. The walls were now covered in flags. I didn't buy any specific flag. Nothing represented a nation; there was no Britain, no Morocco, no France; there was nothing. No religion, no crescent, no cross, no star. I just had a black flag, a blue flag, a red flag and a green flag. Essentially they were nothing more than yards of cloth to cover up the graffiti that lay hidden beneath, but together they were beautiful.

I now sat in a seminar room at a London university.

Slowly lagging behind in my 'studies' for most of the classes I would produce the bare minimum: for some I would actually study and for others I would be too drunk to do anything. One lecturer had already approached me about this and said 'You do lose marks if you do not attend'. One module had become all the more incomprehensible as the weeks went on, and I knew I was bound to fail. I would have simply stopped attending altogether had it not been for *her*.

She sat close to the tutor and was always one of the first to put her hand up to answer questions. She had brown hair and a milky complexion but it was the eyes that I noticed first. Large, dark but calm and sometimes almost sleepy, they gave out warmth that made me feel she was someone I could trust. I did not yet know her name, but I was sure that whatever it was, it was the most beautiful name ever. Suddenly I noticed that someone else was looking at me. From a few seats away a young man of Asian appearance with a goatee nodded his head at me, to which I nodded back and looked away. I did not know why he did this. I looked at the girl again but somehow something in her appearance had changed. I suddenly realised that of the three times I had come to this lesson she never looked at me once. I now hated the girl with her dozy Hiltonesque smile combined with her deathly pale complexion. Suddenly those eyes became vacant discs. With only a few minutes to go before the start of the seminar I decided to leave and never to come back to that room again. I quietly walked out while everyone was still talking and ran up the stairs to the top of the building, looked out towards the cluttered skyline of the City of London, opened a window, lit up a cigarette and calmed down.

It was now evening and I had been sitting in the Student Union all day. Clutching my pint of lager I found myself talking to a French girl sat in front of the slot machines. The first thing I had noticed was the reflection in her eyes from the light of the machine. At absolutely no moment did she ever look at me with those eyes. She did smile, but nothing in her mannerisms indicated that this was anything other than being polite.

I hate it when people try to be too polite with me because it means they want me to go away. In a Parisian accent she kept saying 'ah oui, d'accord' to everything that I said.

Four other girls sat in a circle around a table speaking loud English to each other and giggling uncontrollably. At the count of three they quickly consumed shots.

'Ready! Aim! Fire!' they gleefully shouted.

Upon quickly necking the shot down, they suddenly bowed their heads. It looked like they'd had a group orgasm. A minute later one of the girls started crying and ran off towards the toilets. Another girl followed her whilst the others glanced angrily in the direction of them. I took another look at Mademoiselle D'accord. Her large eyes were distant and ignoring me while she fiddled with the slot machine in silence. I then looked at the table full of loud English women. I took a deep breath and went straight for the bar, bought another pint and sat down as far away from everyone as possible.

I remembered being face down on a pavement outside. Two members of staff were holding me down whilst a third was frantically gripping onto my left leg, which I was trying to kick him in the face with. A few onlookers appeared terrified as the air was pierced with my screaming. I screamed and shouted but do not remember what I said. Soon there was a blue light, the sound of van doors opening and shutting, and the garbled speech of a police walkie-talkie. This time the physical pressure exerted on me was even more intense and a cold, sharp pair of handcuffs placed on me as I was held by the officers and bundled into a cage-like containment area at the back of the van.

I was driven straight to the Royal London Hospital, where my trousers were taken down and a sharp pinprick inserted into my right buttock.

I woke up the next morning sprawled on a white sheet that was hastily placed over a mattress. I was clinging to a pillow that had the letters 'NHS' stamped on it. Next to those letters was a pale milky stain of unknown origin. I recognised this as some sort of shabby, rundown hospital ward with two other equally sorry looking beds. The sky was white and overcast, which added to the bleakness of the place with its grotty, grey walls and smell of detergent. Around my wrist was a green tag with a white sticker that had my name and an assortment of numbers printed on it.

I looked down at my right arm and noticed it was bandaged up like that of an Egyptian mummy. After unwrapping the cloth and picking at the sticky clots of gunk and scabs I could see that one line slashed its way from my wrist to elbow and was held together by nine blue plastic stitches. Four smaller scars cut across it making it look like the five-day marks on the walls of a prison cell. I immediately ran towards the bathroom to wash off the droplets of blood that were trickling through. I opened the male bathroom door to find the place splattered with shit. I retched and slapped my chest three times before running off in search of the female bathroom. It was being used. I was third time lucky with the disabled bathroom.

After having a good clean, I took a careful look at the ward I was in.

In a corner of the room was a man in his mid-thirties who appeared to be embroiled in a passionate argument with himself in Bengali. I got up and slowly walked towards the window. I wanted some fresh air due to the grubbiness of the place but found that the window would not open any more than a few inches. Outside were rows of grim terraced houses. For the first time in a long while I now knew I was feeling sad and wondered what it was I had done to end up here. I turned around and walked out of the ward and spilled into the corridor. The smell of disinfectant was everywhere. It was almost as if the place was nurturing an aura that emptied and sanitised my mind, leaving it as vacant as those very corridors. Out of sheer curiosity

I briefly experimented with the front doors to find that they were fully locked. I entered a TV room, which also doubled as a smoking room, and glanced at the other people sitting there. Most were past forty, corpulent and displeasing to the eye. They were all smoking unfiltered roll-ups. Their bodies were bulging out in all directions like some big, fat, human avalanche. Not one of them spoke to each other but sat watching daytime TV whilst breathing from the mouth. One auburn-haired woman was wearing a large crucifix around her neck. One young, bearded man sat in a corner reciting the opening *surah* from the Qur'an over and over again. In the canteen a neurotic African woman in her late thirties was yelling uncontrollably at the staff:

'DE LORD JESUS CHRIST!!!' she screamed hysterically, 'HE SHALL PUT YOU IN DE FIRE!!! YOU SHALL BURN IN DE FI-YAH, DE FI-YAAAAGHH!!'

She then manically tore off her green regulation NHS top to reveal her big, shiny, black breasts. They bounced around all over the place until a scrum of nurses made her cover up. I sat down on one of the chairs in the TV room and asked someone for a roll-up, which I was passively handed. I lit up and put my head down. One of the fat people said 'hello' to me and asked me how I was. I asked him why he wanted to know and he replied that it was his job. I noticed a badge he was wearing on his shirt. He was a member of staff.

Along the corridors of the East Ham Memorial Hospital were numerous side rooms where it was possible to talk to the staff in private. Later that day a meeting had been set up involving two doctors, a social worker and a head nurse. The social worker did not conform to the typical image of the sympathetic liberal. He was stern, had more of an upfront attitude to his work and had a

Scottish accent. A young female colleague who seemed to make the chair vanish up her arse when she sat on it accompanied a 'Dr Meyers'. The doctor looked at me patiently and began writing his notes. I was wondering what, by just a brief glance, could inspire such frantic note taking.

'Shaza,' he asked, 'now…er…do you know why you are here?'

'You mean you don't know?' I asked.

'I want to hear it from you.'

'Because…I…did…some things…last night.'

I paused for a moment to wipe the saliva from the sides of my mouth. I then slowly glanced around the room.

'Shaza…' he continued, 'Shaza…look at…look at me…now what "things" would that be?'

'Shouted and stuff. I don't know.'

'Well,' he continued, 'You're now on a Section Two of the mental health act. We feel that it's best you stay here on the ward for the time being and…'

'I have lectures!' I protested, 'I'm going to miss them.'

'So be it.'

Suddenly the female colleague intervened:

'What was this about you saying that you've got "rope at home" and that you were going to use it?'

I took a deep breath.

'I was drunk,' I replied.

'...and...Shaza...look at me,' she continued, '...I said look at me...that the split second anyone let go of you that you would kill yourself?'

'I SAID I WAS DRUNK!'

'Shaza,' Dr Meyers continued, 'apparently, during the summer you were hearing voices.'

'No, I wasn't.'

'During a previous check-up you were saying something about hearing voices in German coming from your stereo?'

'Oh, that,' I replied, 'No, he wasn't singing in German; it was English with a German accent and it was all probably nothing but a dream or a false memory or something because something's probably just putting false memories into my...'

I suddenly stopped. The four looked at each other and Dr Meyers resumed writing his notes. I seemed to be digging myself deeper and deeper into this hole with each word that I said. I looked around the room with its whitewashed walls and medical charts indicating something about height and weight. The doctor observed me looking around and carried on writing his notes.

'You're hearing voices right now, aren't you?' he said.

'No, I'm not.'

'So why do you keep looking away? What are they saying to you?'

'Nothing,' I said, 'I'm looking around because...that's what I do. I look around.'

'I think it is best that you stay on the ward for now,' he smiled.

'You know, we may even have tae put you oan a Section Three,' said the social worker, 'which would last up tae six months if necessary. Ahnd if yir nort compliant wi' thaht there's nothing ye kin dew. Treatment comes first.'

Both my father and my step-mother, neither of whom I had seen for some time, were contacted and I was made to show them my arm as if I had done something wrong. My mother continued to look at my arm disappointedly whilst my father shook his head slowly. Am I wrong in thinking that out of all the siblings in the family, the one who turns out the most screwed up tends to be the eldest? We all know that when we try out something new it is normal to get it wrong the first time. On my first day at work I accidentally served someone coffee instead of tea. On my first day at university I spent an hour sitting in the wrong lecture room.

Later on a member of staff told me how upset my parents were to see those scars. He had read my reports and knew that I had moved out at seventeen but as bedtime was approaching I could not make out what he was saying properly. I continued trying to communicate with him.

'What are these scars on my arms?' I asked. 'A scar is a memory. These are memories. They are carved out in front of me and put into flesh. This is a life that is over but I'm living it again and again. I should have said that to the doctor.'

He asked me what I was 'on about' and gave me a tissue to wipe the saliva from the sides of my mouth. I asked him if I was drunk or if anyone had spiked my tea. He told me not to worry because I had been prescribed 'diazepam' and was now drowsy, that's all. He then told me to go to bed and I obeyed without question.

I spent a total of three weeks taking my medication, doing what I was told to do, eating when I was told to eat, sleeping when I was told to sleep, shaving under 'supervision' and spending the day chain-smoking and staring into thin air. This was all relatively easy considering the medication I was put on. The hospital said that they would discharge me but only with the condition that I kept some outpatient appointments. They handed me a new piece of paper and on it I noticed the words *schizophrenic illness* and *dependent personality*.

In the end they decided that it was futile to have me locked up any longer and I will never forget my joy as a member of staff accompanied me down the corridor, swiped his card through the electronic lock and opened the door for me.

I had now been banned indefinitely from the Student Union bar but I could still use the cafeteria and other services during the day if I so wished; I never did. I went to the 'Calcutta House' building of the university to obtain the booklets for my other lectures. Out of curiosity one tutor did ask where I had been for those three weeks. I muttered something about a 'stomach bug' but that I was feeling better now. As I exited the room and walked down the corridor I passed by the girl with the dark eyes again. I looked her straight in the eyes but she did not look at me. She was so pretty that the thought of her not being my girlfriend made me feel very depressed.

I went downstairs to the basement to smoke a cigarette and whilst I was there I looked up to see the Asian man with the goatee. He called me over and asked me my name. He told me his name but I forgot it a few minutes later. He said he noticed that I was no longer attending the seminar and I muttered something about a re-sit. He asked me if I was a Muslim and I just looked at him blankly. He asked me if I wanted to meet some 'brothers' of his at the same place and same time tomorrow and I said I'd see him tomorrow and then left.

Later on I turned round and saw Mademoiselle D'accord waiting outside one of the rooms. She gave a stunned second glance, as if she couldn't believe her eyes. I looked her in those eyes for a split second to notice a mournful look, full of pity, full of sympathy. The Parisian girl felt sorry for me. I turned away and carried on walking. I'd rather not know what she saw that evening.

Chapter 3 – Submission

It was a quiet evening in the smoky basement of Calcutta House. Since discharge I had started puffing away more frequently due to my dosage of diazepam suddenly being withdrawn. I was feeling slightly nervous and had pins and needles at times. On the day of discharge staff at the hospital had told me not to worry since my dosage was not really high to begin with. This was of scant comfort to me and I had been on edge for most of that day.

At one side of the large room were three Spanish girls speaking at 1000 words per minute. With their legs crossed, their books were held under one arm with the other cigarette-laden hand held high in a showcase of effortless multitasking. I made out various words such as *mucho trabajo, por qué, una llamada, pero, cansada, ahora, no sé por qué* but everything else was lost in a blur of speedy lisps and rapid rolled 'r's'. One raven-haired woman had suddenly got my attention, but as soon as she looked towards me I turned away. I was now looking at a man with a large beard who was speaking to the others in the group with a calm voice. He'd already spoken about the worldwide persecution of Muslims after the recent attack on the World Trade Centre. The man with the goatee had kept his promise and I was now in the company of those 'brothers' of his. Of the half a dozen or so young men gathered around the seats, one told me he was twenty-six but sported a fully grown beard and wore a male shalwar kameez. All he needed to do was fling a Kalashnikov over his shoulder and he would have completed a certain look. The others around him were clean-shaven, dressed casually and in their early twenties. What struck me was how young I looked compared to them even though we were all roughly in the same age group. I felt slightly intimidated, as what I'd just said had thrown them into confusion.

'OK, let's start again,' said the bearded one now turning to me, 'You say that you are Moroccan, so we ask you if you're Muslim. You say you don't even believe in God? Prove to me that there is no God.'

I told them that I simply had no reason to believe in His existence.

He then lifted his sleeve.

'Look at this watch I'm wearing.' he persisted, 'This watch didn't just come out of nowhere.'

He then went on to say that if I was riding in a desert and came across a watch I would automatically assume that there was a watchmaker even though I had never seen him.

'To say *watch* is to say *watchmaker*.' he continued, 'You cannot separate a creation from its creator.'

I thought for a few seconds until an objection came to me.

'But the watchmaker made the watch out of material that already existed. He's not a watch creator because he didn't snap his fingers and create it out of nothing.'

I asked about the desert too and if the watchmaker made that as well.

'So where did we come from?' a clean-shaven one in a tracksuit top broke in.

I told him that I couldn't answer that and asked him to tell me where God came from.

'That's not for us to know,' he dismissed.

'Is God perfect?' I asked.

'Well, yeah, Allah is the almighty and can do whatever He wishes.'

'So if Allah created us,' I continued, 'are we perfect too?'

'Yes.'

'So why make any amendments?' I continued. 'Why have operations? Why change anything? In fact, why be judged and go to hell?'

'Allah gave us free will,' some voice broke in.

'Is Allah all-knowing?' I asked.

'Omniscient? Yes!' replied another.

'Is He all-powerful?' I then asked.

'Omnipotent? Yes!' replied someone else.

Now I knew the meaning of 'multitasking' and why I let women do it. I was the only person in the group who didn't believe in God and now my hands were sweating.

'Does Allah know the future?' I asked.

'The Almighty knows everything.'

'So if Allah knows the future, He knows whether you're going to go to heaven or hell before you were even born. So why bother doing anything if everything's already planned out?'

Suddenly one of them lost his temper.

'NOW just because YOU don't understand God this does not mean YOUR standards would apply to HIM! Think about it!'

'Think about what?'

'You're just a human, like me, and YOU can't just deny God because He's too much for YOU to understand.'

Chaos set in and voices flared up as the others in the group tried to calm the man down. The din made the Spanish girls suddenly stop their yabbering and turn around and stare.

Whilst all this was going on another young man in the group was looking at me solemnly. Behind his glasses I could make out two sharp discs staring straight at me. He often nodded whenever I provided an objection to whatever the others said but it was difficult to tell whether he was on my side or theirs. The man introduced himself as 'Abid', and until that moment he had sat on the side of the group, often observing it and sometimes shaking his head disagreeing with what the others were saying.

'So er…'

'Sheza,' I replied.

'So Sheza,' Abid continued, 'where do you stand?'

'What do you mean?' I asked.

'Oh, come on,' he replied, 'you've got to stand for something and not just be against everything.'

'I believe in nothing.' I shrugged, 'I don't see why that should be a problem.'

He was calm and not shouting like the others; he came across as someone I could talk to. I felt flattered by the way he complimented me on how 'bright' I seemed but felt insulted when he said he felt sorry for me nevertheless. Abid said that he would like to speak to me more about my beliefs and invited me to go for a curry with him the next day at a small restaurant on Brick Lane.

The others in the group said that *inshallah* I will come to believe and they shook my hand before I left. My main concern now was to improve my spoken Spanish so that I could find a way of impressing those girls. On the way home I had still been feeling nervous and jittery. I bought a can of Stella Artois and I drank it on the Underground train to settle my nerves. It worked temporarily. Once I got home I spent three hours reading some book in Spanish that I could not particularly remember buying. I noticed how small and skinny I was so I immediately did some press-ups. I suddenly gave up once I realised how much work I would have to put into what seemed futile. I decided to shave the moment I realised that my three-day stubble made me pass for one of the 'brothers'. Still remembering the Spanish girls and their multitasking I attempted this myself. I decided to question the existence of God whilst shaving and I cut myself repeatedly.

Abid arranged to meet at the main entrance to one of the campuses, and from there the two of us headed off towards Brick Lane, after first passing by the flat on Commercial Street that he lived in with his family. As he opened the door he told me to wait outside and went in but had left the door slightly ajar. There was a silence and then I could hear him speaking in Bengali to someone. A few seconds later two ghostly figures covered from head to toe in black slowly and softly crept down the stairs, into a back room, and slipped behind a large curtain and carried on talking to each other there. Abid then said I could come in.

He invited me into his room where he showed me various books about Islam, CDs about Islam, DVDs about Islam, magazines about Islam and nothing else. All of his books were arranged methodically on a shelf in alphabetical order. There was not a crumb on the carpet; everything was tidy, ordered and thorough. He told me he was reading for a master's degree, although I don't remember which subject. I told him that I'd missed a lot of lectures recently. He told me that he woke up early every morning to first wash and then pray, read the Qur'an, eat and attend his lectures on the dot. He asked me about my family and I explained that I fell out with them and left them at an early age. He asked me whether my father prayed and I replied that he did not. He asked whether my mother wore a hijab and I said that neither of them did.

'What do you mean by neither?' he asked.

I then explained to him that I was brought up by my stepmother and did not know who my real mother was and that my father would never talk about her. He looked at me with a glum look on his face. He then nodded and grabbed his wallet and said we should now go to the restaurant.

He wondered why I ate so slowly. I wondered why he was paying for the whole thing. I suddenly became suspicious of his motives as he sat there talking about God, talking at me about God and lecturing me all about God.

'But have you ever seen God?' I asked him.

'So you have to see to believe?' he asked back.

'Well…have you ever seen Him?'

He took a deep breath and calmly exhaled, looking out of the window reflectively.

'I like your honesty,' he replied. 'So you don't actually know what your real mother looks like?'

'What's that got to do with it?'

'I'm just asking,' he replied, 'How do you know your mother exists?'

'Well, maybe she's no longer alive, I suppose. My dad never really…'

'No, no,' he pointed out, 'I asked how do you know that she ever existed?'

'Well, everyone has a mother.'

'But how do you know your mother exists if you've never seen her before?'

'Well, I couldn't have just come out of nowhere.'

Abid sat there slowly nodding his head triumphantly.

'OK, so you do have a mother,' he admitted, 'but why does your mother exist?'

'What do you mean?'

'I mean,' Abid continued, 'what had brought her into existence?'

'Well, her parents.'

'And what brought them into existence?'

I remembered something I had once been told at mosque before I was kicked out.

'This exists because that exists and that exists because this exists, and if we keep going back and back and back we have to come to an ultimate cause, otherwise the past would go on for infinity.'

'Exactly,' replied Abid. 'So God HAS to exist. It would be foolish to not believe in Him.'

'Why can't the past go on for infinity?' I asked.

'Because it can't. Think about it!'

'Think about what? Why can't it go on forever? I mean, people can imagine a future that never ends. If you believe in heaven and hell then you have to. So what's wrong with a past that never began if a future never ends?'

I don't think Abid was used to people arguing with him.

'Well, yeah, you're quite right in what you say about cause and effect,' he replied, 'and you are going to find plenty of Muslims who will try to explain this away but will not be able to.'

He said that it was normal to ask what had created God and that there is nothing wrong with asking that. The response is normally 'but surely God created himself', which, he believed, was just stupid. He said that his belief was that Allah is the creator of everything and everything exists due to Him. He passed some white yoghurt with green mint in it to put on the side of the dish.

'If God is the creator of everything,' he continued, 'it would mean that God is the creator of time itself and therefore God would be independent of it. Sheza, what gives you a beginning, a present and an end?'

I shrugged my shoulders. Abid pointed a finger upwards.

'Time!' he replied, 'And what stops you from being in an infinite amount of places all at once?'

'Time?'

'Exactly! To ask "what created God" is basically implying that God did not create time and therefore is not the creator of everything. So if God created time, and therefore exists independently of it, He has no beginning, no present and no end. He just *is*, not *was* or *will be*, just *is*. Understand?'

I nodded my head.

'The idea,' he continued, 'is basically that you do not need a creator to exist. You need a creator to come into existence. Understand now?'

I nodded my head. He was now smiling. It looked like the mischievous smile that a confident male makes in a club when he sees a beautiful woman sitting alone by the bar and thinks 'I can win her over'. He was looking at me with that kind of smile. We both tucked into what was a mixture of lamb and chicken curry with rice without saying a word.

Normally to shut people up or get them to leave me alone I just agree with everything they say. But I knew I couldn't do this with Abid. I suddenly had an idea.

'What was God before everything existed?' I asked.

'What?'

'I mean, God is the creator of everything, right? So what was God before everything existed? The God of nothing?'

Abid shook his head and asked me what my fucking problem was and why I would still not accept Islam. I replied that he had told me nothing particular to Islam but simply that there could be 'something out there'. He took a deep breath and nodded his head. At times it was almost impossible to guess how Abid was feeling. The eyes can only say so much. He could defend Islam with all the calm of a poker player.

'I don't know whether to call you insincere,' he said, 'but I would call you confused. You don't know why you are here; you don't know where you are a going…why do you stay alive? Do you enjoy life?'

I thought about that question. Normally I had always been led to believe that we don't know why we are here; we don't know what happens after we die, but as we are here let us enjoy life. Such naivety would make Abid smile. I was as sure as hell.

'I don't know.' I shrugged instead.

Abid slammed his palm on the table.

'Basically the way I see it is this. Anyone who is NOT Muslim is going to the fire for ALL eternity, FULL STOP.'

I couldn't argue with Abid because his eyes were smaller than mine. When you have big eyes people think you are naive. People with big eyes always look young for their age. When people treat me a certain age, I behave a certain age. Abid had small eyes and wore glasses therefore he was used to coming across as *wise*. But his eyes were too shifty. I doubt a dog or a cat would ever trust him.

I asked him what his views were on evolution and he laughed when I told him I believed that we share a common ancestor with other primates. He said he couldn't believe how an intelligent man like me could be fooled by such a lie. I wasn't only brainwashed: I was falling for the lies peddled by the 'fundamentalists who hate Islam'. I then kept quiet and finished my food.

'Abid, I know this girl…' I eventually said.

'Yeah?'

'Well, I'm just saying that…well, I don't quite know her. I don't know her name. Er…she's this dark-eyed girl from one of my seminars. And…'

'Yeah?'

'Well, she doesn't seem like a bad person; she seems friendly and charming. I mean…what, she's just going to hell?'

'Is she a muslima?'

'I don't think so.'

'She's going to hell.'

'What about the Mother Teresa?'

'She's met more than her fair share of Muslims in Calcutta yet she still rejects Islam. The Mother Teresa is going to hell. You need to understand. It's not just about doing good. It HAS to be in the name of Allah, otherwise it is a waste of time. Sheza, do you drink?'

I nodded.

'Well,' he continued, 'I don't drink and under Islam alcohol would be banned. But the prohibition of alcohol HAS to be done in the name of Allah. America once banned alcohol but that's not good enough. They didn't do it in the name of Allah. That's the difference!'

I carried on asking him questions. I asked him questions on sex, relationships, drugs, alcohol, masturbation, pornography and he told me the Islamic rules on all of them. So we then went through a list of people, famous and non-famous, dead or alive, and I asked him whether he felt their place was in heaven or in hell. His answers were becoming predictable so after drawing a long list of who is and who is not going to hell I then asked him in the name of fairness whether women get 72 studs in heaven.

If looks could kill…

Offended, he then said he refused to answer any more questions at this stage. I asked him why and he replied that it was useless me finding out more about Islam if I was simply going to joke about it. He told me that I was more likely to burn in hell that way. My stomach had tightened and I no longer wished to eat anything. It was at this moment that I was now yearning for my diazepam again.

He paid for the meal, we headed off, and he then remarked that he was not happy with my fucking attitude but he was willing to overlook my childishness because I was brainwashed by society and needed to find out more about Islam and my duties in life. He said he was prepared to spend a bit more time talking to me because I appeared bright and was therefore worth the effort. Abid frequently talked of his 'brothers' in an organisation called *Hizb ut Tahrir*, of which he was a member, and said that he would very much like me to meet them. I said that I might consider it but I was not enthusiastic now. I shook his hand, said 'bye' and headed off into Aldgate East station. I waited on the platform, walked towards the other entrance and went out again. Still a bit disturbed I went into the Aldgate Exchange pub, said hello to the barman, sat there alone with a pint of Guinness and breathed a sigh of relief.

Chapter 4 – Sanity check

I stayed at that pub drinking until closing time. It was a Friday night, although the pub was not as busy as others were. The groups of people scattered around that I did pay any attention to seemed mostly financial workers from the nearby Square Mile. For the rest of the time I had my head down. I was scared that my only alternative to being alone was to take up Abid's views, possibly even become a sort of protégé of his. I always wanted a big brother.

I looked up and noticed a young Asian woman, smartly dressed in black skirt and white blouse. She was staggering slightly on her way back from the female toilets.

'You alright?' she asked me.

I could see from her slightly drunk eyes that she had taken a liking to me.

'I'm OK,' I said.

'As long you're OK there,' she slurred before heading off back to a table where a white male in black trousers and blue shirt with a black tie gave her a kiss and they carried on speaking with each other. I looked around and realised I was the youngest looking person in the pub, the only one drinking alone and the only one who had the same skin colour as her. I think that the drunk Asian girl was seeing some sort of little brother in me. If I'd been here for an hour just drinking with my head down then I reckon I must have looked very sad and lonely.

I wanted to smoke a cigarette but I had none so I looked at the couple again. They were smoking so I approached them and asked for a cigarette. She smiled and said ‘of course’. The woman then surprised me by delving into her bag and giving me three packets of duty-free Marlboro Lights with a health warning in Greek on them.

‘Hey, these are for you.’ she smiled, ‘You can have them. It’s OK.’

I don’t think she was used to alcohol because I knew she’d regret giving three packets of cigarettes to a stranger just because she felt sorry for him. But I hated situations like these as I didn’t know whether to stick around for a minute and start a conversation out of politeness, which may piss off the white guy because it looks like I’m trying to chat up his girlfriend, or whether to just say thank you and walk off, which is also kind of impolite. I said thank you, smiled at the both of them and then walked off.

I had a few more pints in a mad rush before closing time, before buying a bottle of vodka and taking a train in a random direction. I got off at King's Cross and walked around, threw the bottle against a wall and boarded the next train. Nobody looked at me and I felt invisible. I soon got fed up with shouting at people and sat down quietly. Next to me was a yellow-haired girl about my age talking to a pair of twin brunettes. I rested my head on the blonde's shoulder. I know that when I do something like this the girl will suddenly spring up from her seat and run to the other end of the carriage. This girl sat there calmly talking to the dark-haired sisters in German.

‘Hello,’ said one of the twins. ‘What’s your name?’

‘Sh…Sheza…’ I said, lifting my head up.

As the train rattled its way into High Street Kensington where it was terminating, the three girls invited me to come and talk to them on the platform. It appeared that something about me interested them. They asked me what I had been doing that evening and I said I’d been drinking with friends. (I know you should never say you were drinking alone to people, especially not women.) They kept looking into my eyes and asking me what was wrong and I said ‘nothing’ but they didn’t believe me. The blonde seemed to want to talk to me the most and she brought out a pen and slip of paper. She told me her name but I no longer remember it. She spoke to the other two and wrote down some details again.

'OK, Shei…er…Sheza? Yeah…remember everything that we just said. Sunday morning, eleven o' clock in Piccadilly Circus just next to the Eros statue.'

'What, the cupid with the arrow?' I asked.

'Yeah, that one.'

The blonde gave me a hug and told me to ‘take care’; her friends said ‘goodbye’ and I soon departed out of the station to get a night bus home. It was four in the morning when I eventually got back. It had been a long day so I headed straight for the bed, taking the slip of paper out of my pocket just to make sure that I had not imagined the whole thing. Three German girls wanted to meet me beside the statue. It was there in ink and it had the word *EROS* emphasised in capital letters.

Suddenly I noticed three words at the bottom of the paper: *Meet for church!*

I slowly lay down on the dingy, single bed without taking my trainers off and must have passed out within minutes.

I spent Saturday afternoon in a library, peering out of one of the windows that overlooked a courtyard. I decided that I would meet them the next day. I had nowhere else to go and I really, really was attracted to one of them.

It was a cool and sunny Sunday morning as I sat beneath London's iconic statue of a little boy holding a bow and arrow. I looked up and recognised the three girls as they approached, who were smiling now and not surprised to see me looking different in the least. One by one they hugged me and we all went down Shaftsbury Avenue to this church. I felt some excitement but I could not pinpoint why. I knew, however, that if it were three males inviting me to a church I would not have bothered.

The girls belonged to an evangelical movement in which there was no vicar or priest, just a middle-aged woman in black leather biker gear talking about 'Good News' to a mostly teenage audience. The place was not the old, grey Church that I had imaged but a room located one floor above a seedy bar. The bar was closed to the public that day but there were young, semi-naked women and a few men flocking to that downstairs bar being filmed for something. The noise of feminine moaning and screaming could be heard and eventually both the church and the bar had to close the doors on each other due to the noise each one was making.

The curtains were drawn and a projector turned on with the words to a song. Once everyone started singing the energy was let loose. The girls threw themselves into the music at a faster rate than the boys. Some had their arms up – others were dancing on the spot – but all were singing tunefully and in unison. Some had faces in a trance, others in euphoria, and each song became more and more passionate. After the fourth song, the middle-aged woman addressed everyone with eyes full of zeal. What we are experiencing here was good news, she said, because Jesus dying for us was good news and that's why we call it Good News. She added that sin is a canyon separating us from God and Jesus is the bridge, the only bridge that we can cross to get to the other side. Everyone else shook their head in agreement.

'You OK?' mouthed the blonde in my direction.

I nodded.

Once the woman had stopped her sermon, the singing started again and this time it was louder and more passionate. Nobody in the room looked at anyone else. They were all absorbed in themselves. Suddenly as the minutes went on the boys and girls started singing louder and louder and with more excitement. It was at this point that many of the girls started making exactly the same movements as each other. They sang with raised arms, had their eyes closed as their heads frequently moved from side to side. I noticed the blonde again. She held her arms upwards and I could not see her blue eyes as she had them shut. I wanted to encircle my arms around her waist and make her moan too. We got to the final song and by now each individual was locked in a separate world but rhythmically at one with those all around. The song reached a crescendo that was released with lots of hugging and shaking hands. A few of the girls had started crying.

I stood there in a corner with my hands in my pockets. I looked at the German girl who I was attracted to, again, and wondered what she really saw in that crucifix. She already had the perfect boyfriend.

There was a mixed group of boys and girls who the three girls then introduced me to. They said I was welcome to join them at the café afterwards but I declined. The blonde looked at me again. I wanted to have a relationship with her, not God. The thought occurred to me that I could pretend to believe all of this in the hope that I could have her as my first ever girlfriend. If she doesn't have sex before marriage I could marry her, join her in her song and dance every Sunday and carry on like that. If I pretend to believe in God too much then eventually I will come to believe. The whole pretence seemed so long and arduous, though, which is a shame as she was very beautiful. When I excited the place I got a dirty look from two men making their way out of the bar.

'Bible nutters,' one man said to the other, pointing at me.

I pretended not to hear.

It was getting darker now. I was now walking down a street in Soho with my head down when a female voice suddenly grabbed my attention:

'Are you alright?' she asked. 'You look down.'

A beautiful woman was waiting outside a door that led to a staircase that was illuminated by red lights. She had brown hair and was wearing a dress that revealed her cleavage and most of her legs. I nodded my head but knew that because I only had £4-something on me I was worthless to her.

I carried on walking towards an off-licence to buy a can of lager. I reached the statue of the Piccadilly Archer, sat below it, opened the can and watched the world go by. I felt at one with that statue.

Chapter 5 – The death of Eros

I spent the next following months mostly on my own. At college the only people I attracted were those wanting to have sex in my flat. The only ones I attracted at university wanted me to convert to their religion. So instead I did a lot of reading and had only one more semester to do, and if I passed this I would spend the next year abroad in France. I was now falling hideously behind with my rent. I drank daily. But if I were to pass the exams, then by the time the whole 'repossession' thing went through the courts I would already be in Lyon.

Abid was now showing a more sinister side at the knowledge that I was still questioning his views. He approached me by a photocopying machine and said hello.

'What's that you've got there?' he asked.

'Just some stuff in French,' I replied, 'about the rise of the Front National.'

'Oh,' he replied, 'yes, it's sad. I mean…why does racism exist?'

His grin made me feel uncomfortable.

'What do you mean by that question?' I asked.

'I mean, why does racism exist?' he asked again. 'I mean, what's the difference between white and black, black and brown?'

'Well, yeah, we're all the same species, I suppose.'

'So then what's the difference between humans and cows? Or humans and worms?'

'Well, we humans have cognitive thought,' I replied. 'Cows…erm…'

'Oh, come on. You're an atheist. What's the difference between you and that brick wall? It's all matter, right?'

'Well…the brick wall does not consist of living cells,' I replied. 'I, on the other hand…'

'So what's the difference between you and an apple?'

I paused for a moment.

'The apple isn't aware of its own existence.'

'So what's the difference between you and a dog?'

'I don't know. What is the difference between me and a dog? Abid, why do you keep doing this every time you see me?'

'I thought we were clear,' he replied. 'We've been through cause and effect; we've been talking about so much here and yet you still argue.'

'But you keep coming to me. Is it because of my Muslim name? What about that blonde girl over there? What about those Japanese students in the computer room? What about…'

'I care about everyone. Anyone who wants to listen to the truth will hear it.'

He gave up eventually but not after calling me 'insincere'. In the smoking room some of his brothers called me a 'Kuffr'. They said I was deaf, dumb and blind to the truth and undesirable in the eyes of God. Eventually the entire group contented themselves with the idea that I must be 'a bit bizarre' and hence mentally ill. I told them that I had been to hospital before and I noticed that they were happy to hear that. From then on my rejection of religion was tolerated and all my problems I had only brought onto myself. I immediately told them that many of those I had seen in hospital believed in God and they were suffering from full-blown delusions. I was promptly told that it had nothing to do with religion and that they were simply 'not well'. When I asked why my case would not be the same they would not answer but said that they still believed that my rejection of religion was to blame for all my problems in life. I never did attend that meeting with Hizb ut Tahrir.

I now remained content with simply locking myself away from people, revising and burying myself in various books. This is why I eventually passed the exams and therefore got to a point where it was now my last night in England. I had not yet said goodbye to anyone. I visited my father and step-mother for the first time in ages; they gave me some money and I then left.

Instead of packing, I spent much of my last day in London sat beneath the statue of the Piccadilly Archer. Whilst many incorrectly refer to it as *Eros* many also believe that it is the *Angel of Christian Charity*. It was intended to be neither. It was intended to be Anteros, the twin brother of Eros. Eros is the god of sensual love, lust and desire and represents personal gratification and having something sexual to offer to others: a rather fitting tribute to the carnal areas of London of which the statue is a part. Anteros is the god of 'selfless love', unconditional love, attachment, willingness to make personal sacrifices, to protect and cherish.

Now it was no surprise as to why London tends to forget the true identity of the Piccadilly Archer and keeps mistakenly calling him 'Eros'. It is clear which sibling has won this case of rivalry and for that the Piccadilly Archer remains the loneliest landmark in London.

Chapter 6 – Lyon: city of light

I was on the ferry talking to two blonde English girls. This was the first calm and hassle-free conversation with anyone that I had had in months. I probably found out what universities in the UK they came from and which French one they were going to be spending a year at. I assume I found out their names. I suppose I found out how old they were and what they were studying. I guess they found out the same about me. From the ferry we got back on the coach, and for some strange reason I was able to just doze off for the first time in a long time. One of the girls got off at her destination in Grenoble whilst I was asleep, and the coach terminated in Lyon. There I said goodbye to the other girl and left it at that.

Lyon is the second-largest city in France and has over one and a half million people. Everything was much cleaner than in London and by French standards was extremely functional. The university in London had an 'arrangement' with the *Université Jean Moulin*, where I would be spending the next year. I managed to find the right department and ended up filling in a form with a member of staff. They had already received my deposit that I had sent while in London, so I was handed some forms to give to a residence in an area called Monplaisir.

The staff at the new accommodation handed me the key to a small, barren, white-washed room with a wash basin in the corner. There was nothing on the desk, no books on the shelves, nobody in the room next door, no sheets on the bed, no food in the cupboard and no posters on the walls. I suddenly remembered that I had left most of my possessions back at the flat in London before quickly leaving to catch the coach. A defaced holy book, scratched CDs, broken patio furniture; the bailiffs back in London could have it all to pay off the arrears with. I was now in France and my whole life was contained in one single suitcase that consisted of a few essential items. I wondered what would be left of me if I tossed the entire suitcase into the nearby Rhône. I liked that thought but I could not understand why.

An Englishman called 'Robert' from the International Relations department that dealt with students from the UK told me that it was normal for foreign students to not get too involved with the university for the first two weeks and instead spend that fortnight settling in. I asked him what 'settling in' meant and he replied that it meant becoming familiar with my surroundings. I still did not understand what he meant by this. I hoped that he did not mean living my life in Lyon the way I had lived it in London. In Lyon there were buildings, roads, flats, two rivers, lots of hills, clean pavements, lots of young people, trams and a metro system; I was now familiar with it all. That evening I passed by a supermarket on my way home, bought beer and cigarettes, went to my room, opened the window, lit up and looked out at the skyline.

A few students from England had started a conversation with me after they heard me speaking English with Robert. One explained to me how he got lost on the métro and asked for help. He said that people were willing to help him because he came across as a 'Johnny foreigner'. I noticed that he was pronouncing the names of all the stations wrong. I wondered why people on the métro looked a little more scared of me. I did not come across as an 'exchange student'. My accent was fluid. Nobody knew I was from England unless I spoke English. I did not know I *was* from England until I spoke English. At one point asking for directions I found most people ignored me and quickly moved on. People treated me exactly the same in France as they did in England so therefore I assumed that I must have been perfectly ‘settled in’ by now.

By coincidence I met the students again at a bar in the Vieux Lyon area. It was called the St James Pub and was a place where many English speakers used to gather. Within the space of a few days the students from the UK were all meeting each other, socialising with each other and drinking with each other. Initially I was in the bar on my own, and had been there since the afternoon. I had blacked out at some point that evening and the staff at the bar panicked a few days later when they saw me again. I promptly left as soon as I saw their reaction.

A few days later some memories started coming back. I remembered holding a pint glass, smashing it and pulling up my sleeves. I remembered staff restraining me and throwing me out. None of the English students wanted to talk to me ever again after that moment. I decided that I did not need them. Initially things got worse; I ended up banned from one bar in Sans Souci, two just across the Rhône, and then there were the St James Pub and The Smoking Dog pubs in Vieux Lyon. I ended up getting into a fight with two Algerians in Guilotiére. People were starting to recognise me on the métro. I had now received complaints from the residence and now the university were getting involved. I had barely been here a month.

At the university a young man sat next to me in the computer room. He suddenly struck up a conversation. At first I felt suspicious but I started to relax and he told me his name was Djamel. He had a flair for starting conversations with strangers, a sort of confidence and carpe diem buoyancy, and we would go to the bars together and he would show me around the city. I had barely attended any lectures now but it turned out that he was in one of my classes so I often used to borrow his notes in an effort to catch up. Some evenings we used to drink together and other times we used to skin up and smoke joints in a disused warehouse that had become one of Lyon's largest open-air galleries of spray can artwork. I had found a friend.

It was late one evening and I was in a space on the ground floor of the residence that was used as a sort of study room. I was then approached by a young man and three young women.

'Salut,' said the man. 'Comment tu t'appelles toi?'

'Shez,' I replied. 'Sheza.'

'Chaise?'

'Non...*ehss, ash, euh, zed, ah*...Sheza.'

The young man was a Pakistani called Shezad, who was brought up in France, and out of the three girls, two came from Algeria and one was Spanish.

'You don't look Moroccan,' said one of the girls.

'I said that I was Moroccan?'

'A few nights ago,' she replied. 'You don't remember?'

'You know, Sheza,' another girl asked, 'I've never seen you without a can of beer in your hand. Life...does it please you?'

Suddenly all these questions made me suspicious. What did they want to convert me to?

She had asked me: 'La vie…elle te plait?' In French, *la vie* is a feminine noun. Therefore life is a woman. *La mort* is a woman too.

I nodded because I didn't want to argue.

The four students lived on the same floor as me, and, although considered *'un peu bizarre'*, I soon became familiar with them. Although I was mistrustful at first it soon became clear they were not trying to save me, recruit me or convert me; suddenly I no longer had any stupid questions to ask them.

Late September in Lyon was warm and sunny. I clearly remember a fine Saturday afternoon in the Sans Souci district as I was doing some shopping. My loan had finally come in. At a McDonald's I asked for a Heineken and was asked if I was eighteen. After replying that I was twenty-one, the man looked at me and then reluctantly served me; I decided after that moment that I needed to start filling out a bit. My weight had recently gone down and I was clearly underweight. Suddenly my thoughts drifted away from the supermarket that I was aiming to go to and I noticed something else: a tattoo parlour.

Outside the parlour were two girls looking through the window at the various designs on display. I felt that it might not be right to be talking to them since they looked the same age as me, which meant that they would still probably be in their mid-teens. They both wore baggy jeans, hooded tops, silver jewellery and had dyed hair: one had green, one had pink. I glanced at what they were looking at and commented on one of the designs.

'Ah oui? D'accord,' one of them nodded back.

Suddenly some horrible memories came flooding back and I soon shut up.

'Mais quand meme,' she smiled. 'Bonne journée.'

'Bonne journée,' I replied.

They made their way off.

'Bonne journée. Bonne soirée. Bon appétit. Bon voyage.'

I shrugged off the etiquette, paused for a moment and then immediately went into the tattoo parlour. Asking the man inside how much it would cost to have a certain symbol on my chest the reply was:

'600 balles.'

Balles, the slang term for francs, was a word I thought would now be obsolete.

'C'est combien en Euros?' I asked.

He paused for a moment.

'Euh…quarante,' he replied, 'oui…€40.'

The appointment was booked for the next day, and although I had a lecture on the history of French law on that afternoon, for some reason I just did not see the point in attending. I'd just copy out whatever Djamel had done.

Chapter 7 – The society for cutting up men

The tattoo parlour was small and dark on the inside and had what looked like a large dentists chair hidden behind a black curtain where the actual work was done. The short, burly man who worked there sat fiddling with various objects while talking to a shaven-haired youth who was wearing a white T-shirt and green bomber jacket. Behind the both of them was the black and white flag of La Bretagne. The boy left and the tattooist then said he was quickly going out for a cigarette and asked me if I smoked. As we both stood outside he lit my cigarette and I commented on the Breton flag that I saw draped near the desk. He asked me if I was familiar with it and I told him I'd seen it before. I told him I was from England and he asked me what I was doing in France. I replied that I was studying here.

'Et après?' he asked, 'tu va rentrer en...?'

'Ah oui, je vais rentrer en Angleterre,' I replied.

Something in his nod told me that this was the reply he wanted to hear.

As I lay down on the dentists chair I looked to my left where some of the CDs were stacked. They had names like *Fraction Hexagone, Rudolph Hess* and *Skrewdriver.* By the curtain was a small black patch with a white Celtic cross on it. The patch looked beautiful. Elsewhere were photos of tattoos. The needle went in and the pain started. The music helped make it more tolerable. It was loud thrash metal that managed to drown out the whirring of the needle.

ZZZZZZZHHHHHZZZZHHHHZZZZHHHHZZZ...

Because it hurt I started to think of diversions. One way I could easily get through this was by thinking that I deserved it. The best way was to just sit there silently thinking of as many reasons as to why I needed to be hurt.

My family got fed up with me and I left when I was seventeen. They did not kick me out; I left them. The taxpayer paid for my flat, my social worker, my weekly money, and I trashed it all.

ZZZZZZZHHHHHZZZZHHHHZZZZHHHHZZZ...

I spat and unleashed my phlegm into someone's coffee while working as a waiter. My excuse was that I was only earning £5 an hour. If I am like that on £5 what would I be like if I was earning £500,000?

ZZZZZZZHHHHHZZZZHHHHZZZZHHHHZZZ...

I spent most of the money dad gave me in the last two years on beer and hashish. I would keep hounding him for more money – which I would spend on more beer and more hashish.

ZZZZZZZHHHHHZZZZHHHHZZZZHHHHZZZ...

Whilst drunk on a night bus I got into a fight with an Asian guy in east London and called him a 'Paki'.

ZZZZZZZHHHHHZZZZHHHHZZZZHHHHZZZ...

Those two girls I saw outside this parlour the previous day may still have been in their mid-teens. But if I had the chance what would I have done?

ZZZZZZZHHHHHZZZZHHHHZZZZHHHHZZZ...

I once mentally undressed a Muslim girl in a Mosque who was wearing a hijab. I imagined her still wearing her hijab whilst she took the rest of her clothes off.

ZZZZZZZHHHHHZZZZHHHHZZZZHHHHZZZ…

I am the lowest form of pond life. I am a despicable, demented turd. I am a walking abortion, a failed termination, the one that got away. I am what happens when you fail to separate the wheat from the chav.

ZZZZZZZHHHHHZZZZHHHHZZZZHHHHZZZ…

'Stop feeling sorry for yourself…'

ZZZZZZZHHHHHZZZZHHHHZZZZHHHHZZZ…

Every man, deep down, knows he's a worthless piece of shit. Overwhelmed by a sense of animalism and deeply ashamed of it; wanting, not to express himself, but to hide from others his total physicality, total egocentricity, the hate and contempt he feels for other men, and to hide from himself the hate and contempt he suspects other men feel for him; having a crudely constructed nervous system that is easily upset by the least display of emotion or feeling, the male tries to enforce a "social" code that ensures perfect blandness, unsullied by the slightest trace of feeling or upsetting opinion…the suit on the chimp.
Valerie Solanas, 'S.C.U.M. Manifesto'

I paid up and was given a small tube of lotion and a booklet with instructions on how to keep the tattooed area clean, and told 'qu'il faut JAMAIS JAMAIS gratter les pelures de peau ou les petites croûtes qui se forment'.

The first thing I did after leaving the shop was light up a cigarette.

The weeks went on and winter had slowly started to creep its way in. I had only attended a few lectures at the university now and had no idea what I was doing here. I did regularly attend *français langue étrangère,* however. Some of the Italians spoke with accents so thick that it was hard to tell if they were even speaking French at first. Some of the Chinese girls were so quiet and shy it was hard to tell if they even spoke. Due to Djamel I had made friends with a few Algerians in the area, spoke mostly in French myself and had now well and truly settled in. Sadly, not everyone saw it that way.

Robert wanted to see me urgently.

He had already been informed of my 'troublesome' behaviour at the residence as well as my 'non-attendance' of lectures. I entered the office:

'Ah, hello there, Sheza,' said Mr Sherrat, 'do come in.'

I approached the desk and took a seat. Robert Sherrat was a slim, smartly-dressed man. The look on his face was slightly concerned and unsettled. I already had the notion of being a sort of 'high maintenance' burden ever since members of staff at the university helped me obtain medication, fill in forms, sort out finances and so on. I looked at his face again and into his eyes and I felt like I had done something wrong.

'Shezar, er…we have…received a phone call yesterday from a Spanish girl at your halls of residence.'

I immediately knew it to be 'Clara'.

Sympathetically he continued:

'Well, anyway, she seemed worried. We have been told that you drink heavily each evening, frequently harm yourself, and have even threatened suicide once. She really doesn't know what to do and the truth is neither do we. I mean, the amount that you appear to have been drinking lately, you obviously know that the medication you're on is…pretty hefty stuff.'

I paused for a moment.

'I never threatened suicide,' I replied. 'I don't know where she gets this from.'

He quickly shook his head and waved his hand as if that was not the point he was making.

'You know Monsieur Marée, the regional director of CROUS, is already getting involved,' he continued. 'That means that it is getting quite serious. The CROUS have already evicted students in the past so these are not just idle threats.'

I looked at him calmly. CROUS actually owned most of the student residences in the area.

'So…what are you going to do?' he finally asked.

'Well, the residence set me up an appointment at the regional CROUS office and I've now been appointed *une assistante sociale.*'

'Yes?'

I thought for a moment. This meant that I now had a social worker. Maybe I really had finally 'settled in'.

'And they've arranged for me to have some sort of counselling at a place in Villeurbanne,' I added.

'Well, this is a start, I suppose. I do not mean to scare you here but I must warn you. You've got yourself into a very volatile situation now. You really must tread lightly from now on. You really cannot afford to have any more incidents of this nature taking place.'

There was another brief pause before he continued:

'Oh, and Shezar? Please do seriously consider what I mentioned previously about...going back to London? It may be for the best.'

I nodded my head.

As I left the office my immediate thoughts were that there was absolutely no way that I would consider going back to London; there was simply nothing for me to go back to. On a similar note, however, I had now spent a mere three months in Lyon but was slowly starting to wonder if there was anything for me to stay for, either.

It was that thought that made me pleased to bump into Djamel that evening. At least with a friend here I could say that there was something for me to stay for. First we drank a few beers in a bar near to Vieux Lyon station. The beer tasted weird because it was a special one flavoured with whisky. Behind the barman was an advert for that very beer which featured a man wearing a kilt. Djamel asked why I no longer bothered going to lectures but I didn't know what to say, so I just shrugged my shoulders. He laughed, called me 'dingue' and said that if everyone were like me then nothing much would happen in this world. I noticed that as I drank more my shoulders felt more relaxed and I could maintain eye contact. Djamel didn't seem so interested in the beer. He sat there quietly and he then turned to me and said he needed to roll a joint. We went outside into a nearby alleyway. He said that at first he didn't think I was Moroccan because my hair was so straight. He brushed it with his hand and said it made me look 'asiatique'. I told him this was true and in England everyone thinks I am Asian. He passed me the joint and I smoked it whilst he looked at me and smiled. I smoked some of the joint, passed it back to him, he finished it and we went back in for more beer.

Djamel took an interest in photography and I toyed with the idea of taking as many snaps of certain moments in Lyon as possible to keep with me and cherish, since deep down I now knew full well that something would happen and that I would end up back in London. I barely knew how to hold a camera properly but I wish I could have taken these images.

Those endless steps around the Croix-Rousse district that gave a clear view over the city and the river Saône.

A rainy night in the La Guillotière district as the river Rhône had burst its banks.

Being at the top of the stairs looking down at shoppers and their bags clustered around the fountains inside the large, modern Part-Dieu commercial centre.

A solemn looking girl sat alone smoking a cigarette on the platform of a metro station. Behind her was a blue-tinged advert for 'La Porte Ouverte' with the words 'Besoin de parler?' ('Need to talk?') printed across it.

Two armed CRS officers were on patrol at Perrache station. The colours of the French tricolore on the sides of their shirts contrasting with the black of the uniforms they wore; the pace of their walking, slower than that of everyone else scuttling around going about their daily business.

The next day at university I met Djamel sitting with some of his friends in the canteen. I sat there with them, drinking coffee and smoking a cigarette. Just before he turned to speak to a girl on his side he slipped me a note and asked me to read it. In the note he wrote that he felt excited when close to me and he gave me a description of his body and asked me if it interested me. He told me I had nice eyes and was cute. A minute later, after he had finished speaking I looked at him blankly. Somehow he understood something. He immediately apologised and assumed that I would be interested in him. I asked him why and he blushed, simply saying that I seemed to ignore girls. I told him that girls were ignoring me. He gave me a confused look and explained some things to me.

After a brief explanation I then found out that my tendency to look around all the time might put women off because that doesn't give the impression that I am interested in them. I told Djamel that I tried to maintain eye contact and he called it *'un bon début mais pas assez'*.

He decided to leave his camera at home that evening and asked me to come with him to a bar not far from the Vieux Lyon métro station. It was a small punk and metal venue where young, local bands would get the opportunity to show what they could do. He told me that he could pick up girls and he didn't even find them attractive. While we were there we ended up talking to a small group of people we had just met, and a friend of theirs was sitting on the opposite side of the table as me and was drinking in silence. She had jet black hair and dark eyes, and I suddenly noticed that she was watching me. For a brief minute she seemed to be almost observing me in a way: the way I responded to what was around me; the movements in my eyes and my general mannerisms, which seemed to imply something about myself that I was unaware of. She got up and slowly approached and we soon ended up talking. The conversation was brief, about where I came from, how long I would be in Lyon, the kind of music she liked and so on. Before we had to leave she handed me a slip of paper with her number under the name *Stast*.

Djamel looked slightly pleased with me but he didn't seem pleased with Stast, who he said had *'un gros cul'*.

Chapter 8 – La maison des dingues

One month had passed and I now sat in a corridor with my head down gazing at the squeaky clean, sterile floor. I had been sleeping all day but still felt drowsy, and despite all the medication that I had been given I still felt tense and somewhat overwrought. The anticipation of talking to the doctor in the next room was too great. I was in a much more reasonable state now compared to the previous weeks. Suddenly the door opposite me opened and a Docteur Loche popped his head out and I looked up.

'Monsieur Khawaja?' he quietly asked. 'Entrez.'

I entered the room and sat down.

Dr Loche was a tall man who had a calm and concerned expression in his eyes whenever he talked to the patients. He was greying but with a full set of hair, and although seemingly middle-aged, he gave the impression of being full of youthful vitality. I could easily imagine him, although smartly dressed now, changed into a tracksuit and hitting things with rackets on the weekends. This was obviously someone who looked after himself, unlike the chain-smoking patients who were under his care. Every Monday these patients waited in the corridor to be seen by him, reminiscent of infants waiting for a teacher, guide or protector. Everyone on the ward was subject to His decisions and His rulings, and everyone hoped that He would make a favourable one. His height too, the way He towered over the others, combined with His role on the ward, meant that all the other patients, whatever their ages, would impatiently wait to see Him like a child awaits a father.

I will never forget ending up here, *Le Centre Hospitalier Le Vinatier*, in the Bron area of Lyon. After spending a week on the streets after an eviction, I had spent my days drunk, sleeping in the corridors of people's apartment blocks, watching the trains go past at Bellecour, admiring the station, admiring the trains and admiring the tracks. Somebody found me somewhere and called the ambulance. I was initially talked to at the hospital that I eventually ended up at and told that I was here on my own free will, but before I knew it I was spending day after day in a locked room, was heavily medicated and on a *hospitalisation à la demande d'un tiers*. I assume that the decisive individual in this French equivalent of a 'section', a 'hospitalisation at the demand of a third party', would be the doctor himself. I entered the room and sat down.

'We've contacted the hospital in London,' said Dr Loche. 'Newham?'

The East Ham Memorial had recently closed down and a new, larger place had been built, called the Newham Centre for Mental Health. As soon as the flight was sorted out I would be back in a psychiatric hospital in east London.

'And someone will definitely meet you at the airport.'

'So, doctor,' I replied, 'what's been going on, like, I mean…what is in the notes, the reports?'

He took a deep breath.

'You were certainly disturbed, mistrustful of people, definitely going through a psychotic phase. But I do not think that you are schizophrenic. The hospital in London will have to look into that; it could be a couple of weeks until the transfer. For the moment we have changed your status now to hospitalisation libre.'

'Does this mean that I am allowed out?'

'Non, pas pour l'instant.'

He showed me my report. This was done to assure me that nothing was being hidden away from me and that it was there for me to see if I wished. The report focused not on psychosis or any specific 'psychiatric illness', but on my ability, or rather 'inability', to maintain friendships and relationships, my tendency towards heavy drinking, the history of self-harm, suicide attempts, difficulties relating to the opposite sex and the impulsive 'risk-taking' behaviour.

Robert and another member of staff had come to the hospital with all my belongings after the eviction. Even a member of the French department at the university in London had come all the way to Lyon to find out what was going on. The Université Jean Moulin had also stated that I was an *indésirable*, using those exact words on their report, who they would not consider having back under any circumstance whatsoever.

'I did talk to a girl who gave me her number,' I said to Dr Loche. 'She wanted to meet up at 9.00 pm at Vieux Lyon station on a day when a band was playing at some bar.'

'So what happened?'

'The day we were supposed to meet was the day after I got kicked out of the residence and spent the time drinking and staring at the river. She probably thought that I stood her up, which is better than the truth anyway.'

'Why were you kicked out?' he asked.

'I punched a window.'

'Why?'

'I saw a reflection in it.'

'And why that day?' he asked. 'That day in particular?'

I slowly shrugged my shoulders and he told me to think about that.

'Did you ever have a girlfriend in London?'

'No.'

'And you never saw a prostitute?'

An image of the woman in Soho who asked me how I was entered my mind. I promptly pushed it out and shook my head.

'There were times when you would start shouting and suddenly break into English and then come back into French, go back into English and drift back into French. The members of staff that understood you said you would talk about some girl in London with dark eyes.'

'It's nothing.'

'Doctor?' I continued. 'If I am now much more stable and my status has been changed to hospitalisation libre, can I be allowed out during the day?'

'Non, pas pour l'instant.'

'But…where would I go? That's it. I have nowhere to run away to, anymore. I no longer live in Monplaisir. In the end I would have to return here, to this hospital. Until I'm back in London this is the only place I can go back to. I came to France with high hopes but I have ruined it all. I have spent December here: spent my birthday here. I'm just asking that, for the short space of time that I will still be here in Lyon, before I go back to London, can I just…be allowed out for a few hours a day?'

'And what would you do?'

'Take a few last looks at the city. Vieux Lyon, Part-Dieu, Bellecour, Cordeliers; go for a coffee, maybe buy a few things with whatever I have left of the student loan. I need some new clothes. London is expensive. Maybe I could…'

'Boire?'

'Mais non!'

'You know that some of your psychotic symptoms may actually have been alcohol withdrawal? We even put you on medication and special vitamins because of this.'

I nodded my head, although I had not known this.

For a moment he paused in reflection.

'OK, what we will do is this. Starting from tomorrow you will be allowed out for a few hours in the grounds with the agreement that you return at a certain time before supper. The grounds have a café and a library, so you can easily keep yourself occupied. If this goes well, then next week you will be allowed beyond the grounds until 6.00 pm which means you could go out, go shopping, go to the cinema and...d'accord?'

'Oui, d'accord.'

I did not wish to know why I had jeopardised everything when, for the first time ever, I had everything to lose. The last few days that led up to damaging my own room at a time when I had friends, went to a French university, was about to date, and I had to go and destroy it all. I hope that I would not do this back in London. In any case finding out why I did it would be the key.

I saw out the last few weeks in Lyon in the cold of January. It had started snowing heavily but this was not a problem in itself. On the contrary Lyon still remained beautiful. The difference was that it wasn't as dark and the clocks did not go back for winter like in England, so I would not be constantly fatigued.

It was the middle of January when I managed to book a low-cost flight from Lyon St Exupéry to London Stanstead. A member of staff drove me there and the staff at the hospital in London had been informed of my time of arrival at Stanstead. Immediately I was desperate to leave Lyon and return to London where again I could start again from scratch, since there was nothing for me here in France, anymore.

I do not know what happened to Djamel.

Chapter 9 – Apathy in the UK

I was now at Stanstead airport and wandering around aimlessly with a trolley that had a few bags on it. Suddenly two women, a white one and a black one, approached me and said hello. Both smiled and asked me how I was and I told them that I was feeling tired. They said never mind and that I would be getting plenty of sleep at the hospital they were taking me to, so they escorted me into a taxi that was bound for the Newham Centre for Mental Health. I was admitted to a ward where I was interviewed by a fair-haired Australian doctor. He had already received reports explaining what had happened to me in France and describing my previous history with the mental health service in the UK.

He started asking me questions and kept nodding calmly every time I gave an answer.

'Have you ever attempted suicide within the past two years?' he asked.

'I think so.'

'Do you feel you have difficulty maintaining friendships?'

'I don't think I really have any friends...although I did make one in France.'

'Have you ever been in a sexual relationship before?'

'No.'

Suddenly he looked up.

'Have you ever had a girlfriend before?'

'No.'

'Do you like girls?'

'Yeah.'

'But you've never had a girlfriend before?'

'No.'

He looked up and then quickly started jotting down some notes.

'Do you engage in risky or impulsive behaviour?'

'What do you mean?'

'Do you engage in high-risk activities without fully thinking of the consequences?'

'Like, what consequences?' I asked.

'Such as...do you get into fights with people much larger than you...or into situations where you know you are going to get hurt?'

I still could not answer this question so he moved on.

'Do you drink heavily or use any illicit drugs?'

'I think I might have developed a drink problem,' I replied.

He looked at me reflectively and immediately pulled up the sleeve of my hooded top to see my arm. He gave a poker-faced nod, and I pulled my arm away and he calmly went back to his notes.

'Am I going to be allowed to go out?' I asked.

'You can go wherever you want,' he replied. 'You're not on a section.'

That afternoon I was back in the smoking room of the Calcutta House building of the university. A group of students from the 'Islamic Society' were there. I ignored them and they ignored me; indifference now met indifference.

I soon replied to an advert offering some spare places at a student hall of residence in Bethnal Green. I only had enough money left now for one instalment of rent. I had no plan for what I was going to do afterwards. The doctor formally discharged me from the hospital once I told them I had found a place to live, despite the howls of protest from the nursing staff; all of whom were convinced I would be back in no time.

To make up for my failure in France I now only needed to do a 10,000-word dissertation in French and I could still gain the necessary points needed to go on to the next year. So I would sit there in an empty room with three cans of Tennent's Super (9%) whilst staring vacantly at a blank sheet of paper. I no longer had any energy so if I had too much to drink I would just lower my eyes and sleep. I was now able to spend hours staring into thin air.

For one day I did manage to get out and keep dry but I rarely talked to any of the other students anymore. Many of them were actively involved in an anti-war movement because an invasion of Iraq seemed inevitable now, and outside the campus was a *Stop the War Coalition* stall. I stood in front of the stall looking at some of the flyers whilst sweating and shaking slightly, before asking one of the people standing by the stall for a cigarette. He was a young man who claimed that he had seen me 'a few times around the language department'. He asked me if I was interested in coming to the demonstration. I shrugged my shoulders and told him that I did not know.

Suddenly in front of me I saw *her* again. She was browsing the stall, still as beautiful as ever with some kohl around her eyes. She seemed concerned as if some great issue in life was troubling her at that moment. I swiftly lowered my gaze but then a thought raced through my mind.

'Is it OK if I pass out a few of your flyers, then?' I promptly asked the young man.

'Erm…yeah, sure,' he replied, taken aback by my sudden enthusiasm.

I turned to my side to take another fleeting glance. She appeared even more beautiful than the day I had last seen her. My biggest regret was to walk out of the class that day. I immediately stood away from the stall lest she saw me, and with her dark eyes peering over the form, she then signed the petition. I stood aside the stall with my hands in my pockets and she soon left.

'Is it OK if I sign the petition too?' I asked the man.

'Yeah, feel free!' he beamed.

'Oona' is a female name derived from 'Una', the female Latin noun for 'one'. The Gaelic spelling is 'Oonagh'. According to Irish legend Oonagh was the fairy queen of Knocksheogowna in County Tipperary. She belonged to the nation of Tuatha De Danann and was the most beautiful of all the fairy queens. Although as beautiful as she may have been, she was still able to transform herself into any shape that she wanted. Not a great deal was truly known about her. She was known to be strong, cheeky, determined and she lived in a magical forest together with the goblins and elves. None of her friends had seen her true self before, either, since, like me, it had been kept a secret since she was born. She behaved bitchily and obstinately sometimes but this could easily be taken as a sign of being determined, adamant and strong-minded. Deep down, however, she had a heart of gold and a very carefree spirit. She had also left her e-mail address on the petition, which I hastily jotted down on my hand.

I wrote an e-mail. I told her that it was probably impolite of me to e-mail her but that I couldn't help it. I added that I'd been in the same class as her the previous year and I'd seen her by a stall and I explained how I obtained her e-mail address. I told her that the reason I had jotted down her e-mail address was because I just couldn't let her pass me by. I then sat back and sighed; I had no way of knowing whether she would find it flattering or scary. I wished I had someone to ask to tell me whether I was doing something right or something wrong. I logged off and left the room. I finally decided that the grapes were probably sour anyway. All I wanted to do from now on was drink.

Money had now become a problem and I knew full well that I would be evicted once the next instalment of rent was due. Food was no longer a problem since I had mostly lost my appetite. I had enough money to last me the month, and one of the students would sell skunk to 'fund his studies'. I managed to buy some off him that I would smoke to calm the nerves and ease the shakes each morning.

One evening I sat in my room topless and sweating despite it being February and the central heating being off. I had taken a CD out of a slightly damaged little stereo to find that the music would not stop. I switched the stereo off but yet again the racket continued to screech in my direction, filling me with fear.

In frustration I ripped out the plug yet the violent din kept pouring forth.

I smashed the stereo against the wall before beating it to smithereens with a chair and waking up the entire building in the process.

As I grabbed one of the razors that was lying on the table and bit the blade from the handle using my teeth, blood came spurting from my mouth. I then repeatedly and violently slashed across my abdomen, chest, arms and hands. The cuts suddenly turned white for a split second before crimson blood started spilling all over the place. I took a deep breath before picking up the chair again and hurling towards the window, producing a thunderous smash. The door was opened on the outside by a caretaker and suddenly some officers barged their way in, and I soon found myself under a scrum of men who all weighed much, much more than I did. I was taken to the Royal London Hospital where, again, I succumbed to a needle.

Members of staff from the residence bagged my belongings and brought them to the Newham Centre for Mental Health that I was back at. They handed me a letter stating that:

It has come to our attention that you have a condition for which you require medical treatment; therefore we suggest that the accommodation we provide may not be suitable for you at present.

This was the British way of calling someone an undesirable.

For the first week members of staff at the hospital took it in turns to sit by my bed and anything sharp was taken away from me. If I wanted to shave a member of staff would have to accompany me and stand next to me closely. My laces were taken away; my body was a mass of stitches and I was put on olanzapine, chlordiazepoxide, and antibiotics in case of any infection from the wounds.

Chlordiazepoxide, also known as Librium, is often given to alcoholics to combat the symptoms of alcohol withdrawal. These symptoms can include intense shaking, sweating, panic, anxiety, seizures, hallucinations and delirium. Unlike opiate withdrawal, severe alcohol withdrawal is potentially fatal and many have been known to die from the effects of a delirium tremens. Imagine the worst case of heroin withdrawal you've ever seen, times it by a thousand and you're not even close.

Carlsberg don't do psychiatric hospitals but if they did they would probably be better than anything run by the NHS. As a child I often used to think of 'lunatic asylums' being full of nutters being nutty. The longer I would spend in these places I realised that the grim reality is that of people with histories of suicide attempts, alcohol and drug addiction, domestic violence and sexual abuse as children all locked up together in a place with all the life of a morgue. If one is for those who deviate outwards and the other is for those who deviate inwards then prisons and psychiatric hospitals are truly two sides of the same coin.

The auburn woman with the crucifix was still here. She was constantly there: bulging out in all directions, chain-smoking her unfiltered roll-ups and going on about Jesus. Another patient on the ward decided that he actually was Jesus Christ. I started calling him 'JC' to keep him happy. Eventually, with the help of haloperidol, he started to recover from this delusion and suddenly went through a period of violent depression. He attempted suicide after another patient made the mistake of letting him borrow a nail file with which he slashed his wrists vertically as opposed to horizontally and was taken to the nearby Newham General Hospital; he lived.

In a way I felt sorry for some of these people: lonely, single, unemployed, unemployable, on benefits and living in the E16 postcode of London. They probably felt they had no choice but to convince themselves they were Jesus Christ, the prophet Mohammed, Napoleon, Elvis Presley or whoever else they wanted to be. Everyone is guilty of this. 'Just be yourself' people say, but no one ever does. At a job interview you always paint yourself in a different picture and you always do this on a first date. I felt I was slowly getting just that little bit closer to discovering why I was jeopardising everything.

On one occasion one of the male nurses had me in a headlock as the other held my arms behind my back, and both got on top of me and with the full force of their weight held me down on the bed. A third held my feet whilst a fourth kept shouting – 'Who do you think you are? Who the fuck do you think you are?' – in a thick

African accent. They held me like that for ages whilst I kept shouting at them to go and fuck themselves.

But he asked an interesting question – Who *do* I think I am?

I was soon finding it difficult to breathe and had to struggle to keep my head turned on my side so that I could take in some air. After almost half an hour in this position they let go of me. I was now exhausted and had given up shouting and struggling. As they let go of me it was no longer a great effort to breathe. I had found that all the buttons on my shirt had come out, part of it was ripped, bruises had appeared across my chest and arms, and my belt and trainers had been removed. I remembered what had triggered off the whole incident: I simply said 'Ah, for fucks sake' after one of the nurses refused to let me quickly make a cup of tea as the trolley was being taken away.

I was eventually taken off the section after a few weeks and allowed out during the day again as usual. It was not known what to do with me. My diagnosis was a cesspit of *Borderline Personality Disorder*, *Avoidant Personality Disorder*, *Dependent Personality Disorder*, *Recurrent Depressive Episodes* and *Alcohol Dependence*, and I had soon become the most annoying and troublesome patient on the ward. I now had roughly £20 left in my bank account and no money coming in. There was talk of the hospital discharging me and sending me to the local Homeless Person's Unit. When they did I simply woke up at the St Thomas' Hospital with drips in my arms twelve hours later. There were two drips. One was a clear liquid, obviously water; the other was a yellow 'saline drip' to replace lost salts in the body. I instantly walked out of the hospital before they realised that I had just come out of a psychiatric one. They were sure to transfer me back had I stayed any longer for them to find out that I was now probably classed as 'missing' since the HPU had no record of me either.

Just down the road from the hospital were a bunch of people constantly sleeping outside Parliament Square as a protest against the war in Iraq. I stole a red blanket and a red T-shirt with the words *Give peace a chance* on it (I would use the T-shirt as a scarf.) and walked towards Embankment. It was the early hours of the morning and still dark. I spotted a busy 24-hour shop. Although the alcohol section was out of bounds I still managed to slip a can of K cider (8.6%) into my hooded top and walk out. I kept drifting between Charing Cross and Embankment, since I kept getting 'moved on' by the Underground workers every ten minutes at Charing Cross station. I had only managed to get an hour of sleep at the Embankment, since the noise of cars, the wind going past, drunken revellers swaggering home and the cold, hard concrete I was resting on kept me awake most of the time.

Using my little black rucksack as a pillow I curled up into a ball and disappeared into the red blanket. I had no actual sleeping bag and no secret spot where I could stay away from any disturbance. I was absolutely useless at this and wondered how long I would last. I decided to get myself up to Camden since there was nothing for me in Embankment. Camden was where I met Maria.

Chapter 10 – Maria

I was walking across central London past swarms of loud people taking the night bus home from Tottenham Court Road. I walked past the oil, grease and mustard stench of the sizzling hot dog stands, and passed by the thunderous groans of the refuse vehicles and the noisy conversations in Arabic and French of the men who worked them. The walk had kept me warm during the night but now I wanted somewhere to lie down so I could get some rest. The sky was getting lighter now.

By midday I was sitting by a canal in Camden with a bottle of cheap white cider beside me and the red blanket over my knee. Despite the fatigue with each gulp of cider that I took I suddenly felt a 'hit' of sugar and alcohol that kept me awake. I felt warmer now as the morning sun shone down on me. Again I was moved on from the canal by plain-clothed police officers and had to go elsewhere, otherwise they would arrest me. I decided to sit outside the tube station. There I was approached by a pretty mixed-race girl who appeared to be taking an interest in me.

'Do you wanna buy any methadone?' she crouched down and whispered into my ear.

I shook my head and she quickly got up and moved on.

Every so often someone passing by would hand me £1 or 50p, which I always bought more cider with. I had soon been noticed by some in the area as a sort of young 'newcomer'. I was loud, brazen and aggressive when others told me I was sitting where they normally sat, but a homeless girl would always come and get me out of trouble. She would then wag her finger at me afterwards and tell me to behave otherwise next time she's not going to defend me again. A knife had been pulled out on me at one point outside the HSBC cash point by another homeless man; I was too drunk to care and another woman had to calm him down. The man then left muttering something about 'getting me' later on.

I had only spent the best part of a day here and already I noticed a lot about these men. They took scant interest in any of the girls passing by. Some of the girls were dressed as punks, others more gothic looking, some a combination, and they had all sorts of hairstyles of different colours and wore all sorts of clothes and accessories. Each man drinking on the streets felt that he was not, and never would be, good enough for any of them. These men were just drowning their sorrows in alcohol; they appeared biological dead ends just waiting to die. We all had experiences in the past of being told we feel sorry for ourselves, that friends and family believe that they have to be *cruel to be kind* because our present way of life is *pretty ugly* and is marred by *successive failures*. Yes, they felt sorry for themselves. I felt sorry for myself. This place was now a refuge.

All of the men had at one time been in a prison, a psychiatric hospital or both. Many were ex-serviceman now being looked down upon by the very nation they once fought for. Had it not been for the noise of the passers-by, drinking on the pavements of Camden would have felt like drinking in a monastery.

Suddenly some of the men were pointing at me and joking as another man who was standing up crouched down and talked to them. This man was shaven and wearing cleaner clothes. He wasn't homeless.

'Oi you!' one of the drinkers called over to me, 'Do you wanna job? Do you want money?'

I nodded.

They looked back at the man who took a careful look at me. He turned back at the others and shook his head and walked away.

'Too bad, young man! Says you're not his type!'

They laughed. I took a massive gulp from my bottle and looked away.

It was getting dark now and I was crouched in a corner cradling my bottle. I regained my memory to find myself talking to a young blonde woman with blue eyes, although I do not remember what I had been talking about. She was dressed in grey tracksuit bottoms and a navy blue sweatshirt. Just like me, she was small and slim. Whilst I was talking she was staring at the pavement, nodding and paying attention to every word that I said.

'How old are you?' she asked.

'Twenty-two.'

'Where's your family?'

'I just come out of hospital.'

'Oh…which one?'

Everything I said made her even more interested in me.

'Newham Centre for Mental Health,' I replied.

'I was at St Clements for some time until I ran away. Do you wanna sit near the cash point with us? Them lot over there are a bit dodgy,' she said whilst pointing at the group of young men, who were now giving me threatening looks.

It was true. I felt an undesirable amongst London's other undesirables.

She sat outside another cash point with her blanket, asking for 'spare change'. I no longer remember the name of her boyfriend. Of what I do remember he was Asian and spoke with a northern accent and would also sit by a cash point just down the road from where she was.

'No, Maria!' he exclaimed. 'If he needs to go back to hospital then fine but we can't take him with us.'

'Fuck off, OK?' she said back. 'I know what it's like in there! He can fucking stay!'

'Ah, for fucks sake!' he shouted.

He resumed his post down the road.

'Don't worry about him, OK?' she said. 'He's just being selfish. They ain't taking you back, Sheza.'

The rest of the evening we spent outside the cash point. I would switch between periodically having my head resting on her shoulder and just sitting next to her with my head bowed down, occasionally lifting it to gaze at the passers-by. A few of them seemed to know her. They were people who had just come back from work or were on their way clubbing, and this ATM was always their first port of call.

'This is my half-brother,' she said to one. 'He's just come out of hospital, and I've promised him that he ain't gonna have to go back there.'

Being a 'half-brother' was obvious; it came to her instantly and I accepted it instantly. The difference in skin colour meant I could not pass for a full brother, but having half siblings is normal for most people who I know. I have half siblings myself and they are not the same skin colour as me, either.

A woman who obviously had money, and had obviously talked to Maria many times before, looked at me. I was even asked to show my arms to her; how Maria already knew what my arms were like I did not know. Eventually any money we got – and with me we seemed to get a lot – was shared among the three of us. I did not need much; as long as I could get enough for cheap cider I needed nothing else.

Some of the people would stare at their shoes when they walked past. Others looked hostile. A few women would look at me and produce the same mournful look I remembered so well from Mademoiselle D'accord and the German Christian girl. They were the likeliest to hand me money.

'Sheza, we gotta go now,' said Maria. 'I know somewhere warmer we can sleep the night. We got a sleeping bag you can use.'

'Where's er…?'

'He'll be coming back later. He's gone off to score.'

'To score?'

‘To get my medicine,’ she replied tactfully.

From Camden we walked down past Mornington Crescent towards a council estate near Great Portland Street. We entered one of the side entrances of the block which led up to a fire escape that was both empty and warm. At the top of the grimy flight of concrete steps was a pale, tatty old mattress. Cluttered around it were some empty cans of extra strength lager, a large bottle of water, shards of tinfoil, two lighters and a rolled up sleeping bag. Maria looked at me, told me to ‘stop worrying’ and handed me the sleeping bag. I put down the bottle and wrapped my arms around the bag as I sat beside her. Maria told me that she was once a patient at St Clement's Hospital in Mile End; she had gone through repeated ‘breakdowns’ where she would not eat or sleep for days and had to be put on a section of the mental health act. During these periods she would become angry at the world, go through mood swings, and remain immobile for long periods where she would neglect her appearance and simply stop caring about anything. She let me put my head on her shoulder. As soon as I did this she put an arm around my waist. It was the first time anyone had done that. We heard a door opening and the sound of steps; her boyfriend had arrived. Maria gave me a kiss on the forehead, got up and started preparing the mattress, clearing away the clutters of empty cans and bottles and pulling out a roll of supermarket tinfoil.

I watched attentively as her boyfriend produced a brownish substance and handed half to Maria. They both spread it neatly across a piece of tinfoil. They used a lighter to burn under it, and using a straw-like implement, also made of tinfoil, they inhaled the stuff instantaneously.

'Sheza. If I see you doing this, I'll cut your head off,' she warned.

I nodded my head.

That night I sweated profusely under the sleeping bag, but I kept sipping from the bottle of warm cider and the sweating soon stopped. I was repeatedly woken up by the sound of female coughing, but her boyfriend seemed to have no difficulty sleeping through these bouts of coughing at all. Something was physically wrong with her.

The next morning was spent getting ready. The next few days were spent going to the cash points together, splitting off onto three different ones and joining each other a few hours later. Every hour I would go and join Maria for a few minutes and before I left she would give me a kiss on the cheek. I would then go to a shop, buy a can of something and resume my position outside the cash point. Maria's boyfriend was mainly concerned with the amount I drank and that it didn't look good if I was begging with a can of alcohol by my side because people were less likely to feel sorry for me and hence less likely to give me any money, but Maria would continue to defend me, frequently making excuses for me. In any case I was still getting more money than the two of them combined. One brown skinned woman in a hijab handed me a fiver and smiled at me dolefully. Muslim women seemed, on average, the likeliest to take one look at me and hand me money.

After a few hours Maria and I always went back to the flight of stairs, leaving her boyfriend to 'score some more gear'. I had always thought that living with heroin addicts was like living with a bunch of pet cats. They sleep around all day doing absolutely nothing, only come to you when they want something and then disappear again. I cannot understand why Maria was not like this. Maybe something about me was changing her; I certainly became the vulnerable little sibling to suit her needs, too.

Later the boyfriend had gone to score again as they seemed to have more money now, leaving just me and her again. Maria's eyes were drowsy and she smiled at me. I took another sip from the can and she told me to 'come here'. I approached and she planted a kiss on my cheek. She then planted a kiss on my forehead, stroked my hair and rested her head on my shoulder and closed her eyes. I sat in front of her on the step below her as she clung to me without saying a word. I must have nodded off briefly because I remember waking up still in her arms.

I understood this whole way of life and what had brought us all here, now. We were unable to see the world beyond ourselves because the world beyond ourselves could not see us. We were trapped inside ourselves. To succeed in this world you have to commodify yourself and have something to offer. For Maria people were just a financial source for her next fix. In a sense, she was right. Maria didn't want to prove herself to anyone anymore. People always gave me more money than the other two outside the cash points. This was partly because I looked young and 'vulnerable'. Others saw a common skin colour and assumed I would have more in common with them. For others I was somehow more 'innocent' than the other two and therefore more 'deserving' when begging. None of this mattered anymore. As long as I got their money in the end, I'd be whatever they wanted me to be.

I realised that I was running away from an identity. It was clear to me why Maria's boyfriend was not so hostile to me. I was not seen as a 'threat'. No woman had yet ever loved me the way a woman loves a man, but the way a woman loves a child. I grew up with the idea that the man is always the *perpetrator* and the woman is always the *victim*. The man is always simple and the woman is always intricate. That the man comes off the rack ready-made, whilst only the woman has emotions, sentiments and uncertainties in life. I could already see that when girls at university would hang around in large groups, binge drinking in the evenings, secretly deep down they felt that this was the case. This is why as individuals women would keep away from me but in large groups they would talk to me. I always hated large groups so I would subsequently keep away from them. I felt that they held resentment towards men that would make me resent myself for having such hostility, aggression and anger. I was a stereotype of everything I did not want to be but felt I had to be: the drunkenness, the fights, the arrests, the bannings, the restraining, the handcuffs. If women were to hold men in such a low regard then I was afraid I did not wish to be one.

Maria was still resting her head on my shoulder. Her eyes were glazed as usual. For a moment, however, a brief moment, I felt like I was the one doing the protecting. I was no longer the 'little brother'. I finally felt 'needed' and not 'in need of'. I planted a kiss on her cheek. I could not remember having felt this close to anyone before.

I could hear the sound of footsteps, meaning her heroin delivery boy was back. I thought of the gear. Afghanistan's finest. Here we were at the end of its journey, the closing stages of that trail, the final conclusion, at the top of a fire escape in north London surrounded by lighters, tin foil and cans of cheap cider.

That night, Maria's coughing grew worse. At one point she started retching and eventually vomited.

I was told by the both of them that they spent a few days at a hostel now and again where it was possible to get a hot shower and a warm meal, and Maria insisted that I come along. I felt I could do with this. Sometimes when they would stay on the flight of stairs I would go for a walk and come back later. I do not need to tell you why. Somehow I was jealous. But if Maria was to be my sister then I could not afford to be jealous. I tried not to think about it. To pass the time during these moments I would buy a can of Tennent's Super and make a few roll-ups and watch the world go by.

One of those days I had blacked out after drinking too much and I suddenly regained consciousness to find myself screaming and shouting in a hospital bed.

'Fuckin' bastard!' I screamed. 'Fuck you!'

'Now, calm down, alright?' ordered a police officer. 'Calm down!'

I had regained my memory to find I was already screaming at two officers who were in the room. To my side were metal rails.

'Fuck off!' I shouted.

'Yeah, yeah, keep going!' he replied.

'I'm hungry!' I shouted. 'Can I have that sandwich over there?'

‘No, the nurse needs to stitch you up first.’

On the side of my neck I could feel some sort of cut, or possibly a wound, being prodded by some metal implement and soaked with cotton wool drenched in something. The nurse then produced some white strips that she placed across the area. I noticed one of the officers clenching his teeth as he saw it. I remember nothing of the circumstances that led up to this.

‘Er…She…er…Sheheezer is your name?’ asked one of the officers. ‘Well, we’re taking you back to the Opal Ward. You’re a patient there?’

‘No!’

‘We’ve got a report here that…well, you’ve been put on a section now.’

‘You can’t take me there. My sister’s probably wondering where I…’

He said that I was on a section, that I was an inpatient at a psychiatric hospital, that I was classed as ‘missing’, that they were going to take me back and that there was no point in arguing. I wolfed down the sandwich and was handed two little blue pills to take and I knew that if I refused them then I would be injected. I had jeopardised something yet again. I now knew I was re-enacting something.

Exhausted, I was handed over to the ambulance staff, put in the ambulance and made to lie on a small bed with a red blanket. I felt my neck. By now the area had dried and the entire side of my neck, the flesh, felt as hard as a plaster cast. I was taken back to the ward and had to go through the same procedure all over again:

the Librium, the anti-psychotic medication, the constant observation, removal of all 'sharp objects' from my presence.

The whole of summer was spent locked up on the ward. Not a lot happened. The first few weeks drifted past for the heavy medication I had been administered. I was eventually allowed out as long as I was accompanied by a member of staff. I ran away one more time and returned straight to the block of flats. No one was there. It had been many months since I suddenly disappeared from Maria's life. By this time I had been looking slightly healthier. I had gone a long time without a drink and the welfare officer at the hospital helped me apply for benefits so I always had a small amount of money on me. I left the flats of Great Portland Street and made my way to Camden, where I had a feeling they would be.

I instantly recognised one of the dark-haired girls begging outside a cash point. She had once even stopped me from getting stabbed outside Camden Tube. The girl looked sullen and extremely inebriated.

'Excuse me,' I said to her. 'I don't know if you remember me. I'm er...'

'Hello there,' she replied. 'I've seen you somewhere before, haven't I?'

I nodded and immediately made for the off-licence and bought two cans of White Ace (7.5%), one for me and the other for her.

'Do you know where Maria is?'

'Who?' she asked.

'Maria: small, blonde, my size, has an Asian boyfriend, often seen outside this cash point. Maria?'

She thought for a moment and told me that Maria was dead; however, I did not wish to take her word for it since she was drunk, had dilated pupils and was stuttering incoherently at times.

It was getting rather late now and I just remained in the area eventually getting drunk, as usual, to the point of blackout and memory loss. I decided to make my way back to the flats. Even if no one was there I was better off going back and sleeping on the mattress myself.

Whilst I was in Mornington Crescent three young, tracksuited chavs asked me for a cigarette. I said that I didn't have any more. One of them stood directly behind me. I moved away but he carried on standing directly behind while the other pushed his way in front of me breathing vodka in my face. I swung a punch, hitting him on the forehead, and ran away but I was suddenly struck across the face. I curled into a ball and repeatedly received blows to the head and body coming from different directions simultaneously. I immediately protected my head and borrowed into myself hoping that they would give up and go away and that none of them would produce a knife. The three carried on shouting 'fucking come on, fucking come on, you fucking cunt; come on, fucking come on' before giving up and going away. I sat there with my head down by the shop shutter that I had collapsed against. I felt the right side of my face and spat out some blood from my mouth. With my tongue I could then feel that a front tooth was now missing. I found the remnants of the tooth. It looked so small, petty and insignificant on its own that I flicked it into the gutter. I then carried on with the long trek towards Great Portland Street. As I reached the flight of stairs I noticed someone else was using the sleeping bag that I once used. He had heard me coming up the stairs and woke up. On the mattress was Maria's boyfriend and no one else.

'Shez?' he asked. 'Where you been all this time? What happened?'

'Who's this?' asked the other man.

The boyfriend quickly explained something about '…and Maria used to look after him' before turning back to me and asking me what had happened. I explained the drunken blackout and the scars on my neck.

'Yeah, I figured something like that would've happened,' he said with absolutely no surprise.

He looked at my face again.

'Shez, and what happened just now?'

'Just three guys,' I said, 'they been drinking, I been drinking. They go for a night on the tiles and they'll just…show off about it tomorrow.'

I remember the sudden silence before he finally spoke.

'Shez, you know er…Maria.'

'Yes?'

'She's gone.'

I looked at him.

'She's er…gone beyond here.'

'Why don't you just say it?' I asked.

He remained quiet for a moment.

'Did the hospital allow you out?'

'No, I ran away again.'

'Shez, Maria's gone. I think it's best you go back to hospital.'

He invited me to sleep on the flight of stairs that night and tomorrow I would go back to hospital.

'Shez, you can sleep here on the mattress. Don't suddenly go anywhere, yeah? Stay here and we'll see about getting you back to hospital tomorrow.'

I remained there on the side of the mattress thinking of her. It dawned on me that she may have died thinking I had just run off. It also dawned on me that she may have known that she was dying all that time. I wondered whether this could have been why she had such a desire to 'look after' someone. If Maria's life was a half finished jigsaw puzzle, then I must have been the extra two or three pieces before she finally gave up with the whole thing.

I did briefly wonder where, if buried, she may be but the thought soon struck me as unimportant. I wondered why I was now feeling scared. I looked at the other two. They were asleep as if nothing had happened. Her death was insignificant; I could even hear them snoring. After a few hours of staring into nothing, I quietly got up and left whilst the other two were asleep. It was now dawn as I spilled out of the block of flats and into the car park where everything seemed to be in a twilight state.

I sat outside Great Portland Street station for an hour or so until the trains started again, and waited on the platform. As the train approached I suddenly felt scared again. I now knew that the thought I was having was one of wanting to join Maria. If she was in heaven I wanted to be there too. If she was in hell I wanted to be there too. If she was reduced to ashes I wished to be reduced to ashes. If she was nothing, I wanted to be nothing. But the one place I did not want to be was here, alone and free. I realised that I was so free now that there was nothing that has ever stopped me from, nothing to stop me from, nothing will ever stop me from…I looked at the tracks again, looked at the train, the speed it was going, and took a deep breath. For the first time in my life I felt free.

I just wanted to go back to hospital and they immediately took me back in when I pressed the buzzer.

I simply had to stay in hospital, eat when I was told to eat, sleep when I was told to sleep, wake up when I was told to wake up, take my medication when I was told to and speak when I was told to speak. I passively accepted what was given to me in hospital and for that I was eventually given a room at a home for former psychiatric patients in east London, where the house manager was a woman called 'Halima'. My parents had resumed contact with me but nothing seemed the same anymore. I was twenty-two years old and now living on benefits; I now had cleaner clothes, however, took care of myself and had an address. The plan would be to recuperate for a year and then possibly return to university and put this whole episode behind me as if it had never happened.

Maria's life was so brief it might as well have never happened.

Chapter 11 – Drunk in Johannesburg

It was a warm, sunny morning as I walked along the path that divided the immaculate lawn in two and approached the veranda of the small, white house to get inside. The room indoors was messy, humid and ramshackle with the wooden walls blotchy with mould and damp. Although nicely painted on the outside, from the inside it looked the sort of flimsy dwelling you could demolish with a cricket bat.

'Where's Halima?' I asked.

Suddenly I felt tied up, drugged up and unable to move. The face of a middle-aged African male was over me and he was reciting what appeared to be a Christian prayer. I suddenly remembered that Halima was a Jehovah's Witness. Suddenly I felt forced into a bed, tied up, drugged up and unable to move. The face of a middle-aged African male was over me and he was reciting what appeared to be something about 'The Lord'. I felt sedated and something was being inserted into my nose. I tried to muster a sound to tell everyone to go away but nobody would listen to me and suddenly there were more people scattered around the room. The old black man continued his reciting and I tried repeating his words but I could not. Standing helplessly in the background was a woman looking at me mournfully.

I managed to run free and get away from the house. I was now somewhere in central Johannesburg. Not far off, large groups of black girls in uniform were on their way to school. Sitting on the pavement were two women talking to one another, one of which was carrying a baby on her back. What I then remember was the sunny blue sky, the skyscrapers and the stream of cars on motorways that had seemingly endless carriageways. I managed to find a petrol station which was owned by some white-trash beer-and-biltong family and had bulletproof windows and a black security guard. I bought bottles of a beer called 'Castle'. Whatever had happened during this drinking session had brought me back to a hospital again. At the other end of the ward were a whole host of alcoholic drinks, all which filled me with fright. At certain times I felt like I was being moved around, often on my side. Sometimes things were being put inside and outside of me. Like in France, I thought to myself, people in South Africa are going to get fed up with me eventually.

'The boy's father is here,' said a voice.

My father had come all the way to Johannesburg to see me but I do not remember actually seeing him.

I was discharged from the hospital, or I just walked out; I forget which. I simply promised myself that I am not going to drink but soon promise myself that I will simply cut down, and somehow it never happened. I kept getting drunk, helpless and at the mercy of others even when I could not remember drinking. I could not seem to understand where I was getting all the rands to pay for this. I found a bar in a slightly nicer northern suburb of Johannesburg where a blonde soon told me:

'Yeah, we will serve you...but no more than four.'

I agreed and soon went elsewhere afterwards.

I was staggering around one of the world's most dangerous cities, loud, drunk, aggressive but helpless, at three in the morning, and even the robbers, murderers and thieves did not seem to bother with me; this was hell.

I eventually returned to the house in the suburbs. Halima had now gone back to the UK and the house now had new owners and I explained the situation to them. The place had now actually turned into a brothel but there was a Chinese restaurant next door too. It turned out that the restaurant joint owned the brothel as well, although they were very discreet about this. The women there talked to the management about letting me stay temporarily.

‘Ah, come on, the kid hasn’t got anywhere to go; we just put him up for a few nights until he goes back to England, that’s all,’ said a girl in a short skirt, who looked like Mel B from the Spice Girls, only she had an Afrikaans accent.

They agreed, but the big black guy who worked as ‘security’ for the girls remained suspicious. He belonged to a ‘syndicate of carjackers’ who were currently at war with the police. He saw me as a threat who could ‘go blabbing’. So he constantly sat next to me whilst I slept. By my bed were some lights. These lights represented the parts of the suburbs and townships where the police had been placing CCTV cameras in an attempt to win the war against the robbers and carjackers. The man was sitting next to my bed with a machete and three lights had gone up. He had threatened the police that if one more light went up (which would represent a new camera being installed) he would chop my head off. I remember thinking that if the authorities are going to put up more CCTV cameras in the townships, they could at least wait until I have left the country, first. Fortunately the light did not come up.

'Relax,' 'Melanie' said to me, 'he likes you really; if he didn't he would have chopped your head off by now.'

With those comforting words I went to sleep. I woke up to find that the guard himself was asleep too. I tried to reach for the machete but I could not lift my head for more than a few seconds.

The return to England was not so bad. It was actually on a ship from Cape Town, although I did not get to see much of the city. I could do nothing on my own accord and everyone was just rushing around doing everything for me. The ship started moving and we started hovering towards a room with white lights. We got to Portsmouth and all the immigrants and asylum seekers started leaving one by one. A Chinese girl looked me in the eyes and said:

'Sheza, you don't know how lucky you are.'

She kissed me on the forehead and then jumped off the ship straight into the water. Everyone started panicking but she could not be found.

I had not been able to talk properly recently. Somehow I tried to make a movement out of my throat but no sound could be produced. It was about this time that a smouldering hunger had started burning away from the inside. At times the burning in the stomach would grow so unbearable that I would muster all my strength to pull and grab at anything I could see and try to bring it towards my lips only to find nurses panicking and immediately taking it away.

Halima appeared again. I tried to talk to her but my throat could not produce a sound. Later on, a white male nurse who was sat beside my bed had left. I tried to reach for the small bottle of cola that he was drinking from. He frantically ran back to stop me. Later on I was reaching for some water. I had a drip in my arm and the previous stuff up my nose was no longer there. I reached for some plastic drip-like bag that looked appetising since it was of a yellowish colour instead of the clear liquid drip on the other side of the bed. I tried to bring it to my teeth so that I could bite from it to drink it; immediately a blonde nurse came and snatched it away. My head felt so heavy I fell back onto the pillow.

'You can't drink that,' she shrieked in an English accent. 'That's dirty water. You don't want to drink dirty water, do you?'

A moment of clarity came to me one morning. I gradually lifted my head from the pillow and turned my head towards the window. It felt like I had already done this the previous day but now I had noticed things that I had not noticed before. I could make out the grey, gothic hue of the window sill. Above it was a pale, overcast sky suggestive of northern Europe and not South Africa. Various nurses were walking up and down the ward, talking, laughing and getting on with their tasks as I lay there mute and helpless. One young woman, smartly dressed in a pale nurse's uniform, suddenly noticed that I was awake and indicated this to a burly middle-aged male.

I almost fell as the grey-haired man helped me out of bed and gently lifted me into a chair. He wheeled me into a bathroom where, upon looking into a mirror, I slowly rose to come face to face with a harrowing sight. A pale and emaciated wreck stood in front of me, some of the head had been shaved and there were two surgical scars making tracks across it. The cheeks were sucked in, the cheekbones sharp; the eyes had a yellow tinge and were rendered huge and panic-stricken by the meagreness of the face.

The hospital gown I was wearing was unlaced from the back so I could be washed. Now naked I noticed another large surgical scar down much of my abdomen. Touching the flesh around it was like pressing against wood. I did not want to know how much I may have been weighing at this moment. The man made me sit in a special tub where I was gently washed over. I wondered for a second whether this was the hospital I was born in.

After I was helped back to bed he handed me a small carton of a bland, tasteless drink that had the consistency of milk. I sipped it slowly, mustering up the energy to complete a full four sips before putting the half empty carton down. The grey-haired man reappeared and patiently looked at me:

‘Again, do you know where you are?’ he enquired in a mellow Irish accent.

‘Am I still in South Africa?’ I asked.

‘Er, no,’ he replied calmly, ‘you’re on the Sophia Ward of the Royal…London…Hospital in Whitechapel. You jumped in front of a train at West Ham station.’

The man was now talking to the nurse again. She had dark hair, blue eyes and also spoke with a soft Irish accent. She smiled as he commented on some piece of news in a newspaper that they had both been skimming through.

'Where am I again?' I asked.

'The Sophia Ward of the Royal London Hospital in Whitechapel,' she replied instantly.

The girl smiled at me and they carried on conversing quietly.

Chapter 12 – Getting 'one under'

As the days went on more memories came back. I now knew it was November 2004 and that I was twenty-three years old. I was supposed to be back at university since I had re-enrolled in September. I must have been drinking at university when this whole thing had happened. I do not know what I was doing at that station in particular. As far as I knew I used to pass by it on the District Line but I had no direct business there. London Guildhall University had now merged with the University of North London to become 'London Metropolitan University'. It was when I finally came back to university that I started on a sort of violent alco-binge that even street drinkers did not do and must have lasted barely a week before this happened. I remembered having a Moroccan mother somewhere. I remembered that my name was 'Sheza', although a few days later I remembered that, officially, my name was spelled 'Shehzer'. I remembered that I was living at a house in east London where Halima, a middle-aged woman from Ghana, was the house manager. To this day I remember nothing of the two weeks that led up to the incident. There may be other things I do not remember but obviously I may never know.

I looked to my right and saw what was written beside my bed:

'Name: *JB Quebec Unknown*'

I asked a nurse what this meant and she explained that at first the hospital did not know who I was so they had to use some temporary identification, but I did not have to worry about it because they had all my details now. She offered to rub it off but I asked her not to. For almost a week, those letters in blue felt-tip pen must have served as my new identity. She explained to me that the 'JB' stood for 'Joe Bloggs', the British equivalent of 'John Doe' or 'Pierre Untel', and that the 'Unknown' meant exactly that. I asked why there was a 'Quebec' in the middle and she said that was a mystery to her too. Again the nurse offered to rub the whole name off but I asked her not to. It served as a reminder that I could literally have died an unknown. Quebec remained a mystery.

The next day I found out that the reason they temporarily stopped feeding me was because a liver laceration meant that I needed an emergency operation. Not shortly after, an infection had spread to my throat, and, if fed, there was a risk that the food would go straight to the lungs and not the stomach. Suddenly I remembered the bag containing the yellow liquid. Which death is more dignified: choking on your own urine or having your innards scraped off the train tracks? I was also told I had jaundice now. Of all things I had to 'lacerate' it had to be the liver; still, at least it was not the heart.

I slowly started walking up and down the ward occasionally as the days passed by. The man in the next bed was Russian. He'd got into a very bad fight and he required an operation on his head and had stitches running down it, too. He had a very beautiful blonde girlfriend who came to visit him with some friends and they all crowded around him speaking Russian. They looked at me sitting there alone and offered me a slice of pizza out of the numerous boxes they'd brought with them. I nodded and out of the cluster a dark-haired male, who looked more like a fair-skinned Chinese, came to me, handed me a box with one slice in it and I said thank you.

As I ate I looked down at the white plastic bag full of my clothes. They served no purpose anymore. The navy blue jeans had been torn with scissors, as had a dark green jumper and white T-shirt. My little black rucksack was there too. Inside there were various sheets of paper with reference to politics and international relations. There were sheets and sheets of handwritten notes in French. I understood every word. Tout de suite je me suis souvenu que je parle français et que j'habitais à Lyon dans le passé. I wondered how long I had been able to speak French and I soon remembered that I could speak some Arabic too. I seemed to remember some Spanish as well although at first I could not figure out why. Not long after, the memory of three pretty Spanish girls came to mind. I then remembered that I used to teach myself Spanish sometimes in the evenings. I then remembered the Islamists, the Christians, Djamel, Oona, Maria.

The 'Quebec' was no longer a mystery any more. They, whoever *they* were, needed some way to separate *me* from the other JB Unknown's. Someone had gone through the bag, seen the notes in French and thought of a name. In the space of a few minutes, I'd been given a whole new identity. At the bottom of my bag was a cigarette packet. I was allowed downstairs to smoke and almost felt sick after a few drags.

If you were held up on the eastbound District Line on the 18th October 2004 towards midnight, then I am sorry for the delay; it was me. I sometimes think of the driver himself, who may have ended up traumatised for the rest of his life. The term for this is 'Person under Train', although in colloquial terms Underground drivers call it 'getting one under': an occupational hazard that almost every Underground driver goes through at least once during their careers. This particular time I was brought to the Royal London in an emergency helicopter and not an ambulance.

On the New York subway a ‘one under’ is called a 'track pizza'. It should be easier if the person dies; all that needs to be done is to scrape the person off the tracks and resume service as quickly as possible. If the person is still alive then the delay will be for much longer. The survival rate is surprisingly high but many do not survive intact.

To this day I observe people on the Underground. These people are waiting on the edge of platforms, inches away from the approaching train and feet away from electrocution, yet they think nothing of it. In the modern world we dance with death on a daily basis in a way even our ancestors did not. The death of our ancestors did not involve fragility of the organic in the face of technology, of warm flesh and blood being stamped out by the steel monster roaring past. My destruction was not completed due to the human face at the front. I owe my life to another life.

My father had come to visit me a few days later. He was a man who didn’t look like me. His skin was lighter than mine, although I knew that this was because his mother was white and his father was brown. I found out from him that an imam had been told that a young *Muslim* had been involved in an *accident* on the London Underground and prayers had been organised. Eventually another imam briefly told others about this person, and it soon snowballed into hundreds praying for him in a mosque down the road from this very hospital on Whitechapel High Street. Soon his family in Morocco did the same and were praying for him in Casablanca at the world's fifth largest mosque. It felt like reading a newspaper article about someone you know and thinking 'you've got it all wrong'.

'After all this do you not believe that there is something out there watching over you?' asked my father.

I told him that I was sorry but, no, I did not. There was an Underground driver who hit the red button, emergency medical crew that arrived, emergency helicopter services that took me away, surgeons at the Royal London who carried out operations, but no God was present. He did not bother arguing. We'd been through this many times before.

'Shehzer,' he continued, 'you know I can't see you drink another drink ever again.'

'I know.'

'You say that now. What about when you start to recover? You gain weight, your voice comes back and everything goes back to normal. What are you going to say then?'

'This is normality.'

'What about implants?' he continued.

I asked him what he meant by this.

'Implants!' he yelled. 'Antabuse implants so that you would be unable to pick up another drink because if you do you would feel horribly sick.'

My dad looked scared.

'Do you know what we've been through?! Two weeks we didn't know if you were to live or die! They even offered counselling for the kids in case their older brother was to die!'

I remembered that I had a brother who was approaching adolescence. If I had died, within a few years he could create a story out of that which he could say to girls to gain sympathy and get laid. Suddenly I felt jealous that he could have a story to tell and not me. I said nothing of this to my father. His identity was too grounded, his values too strong; therefore trying to reason with him was pointless. He now had a lump in his throat while he was talking.

'Shehzer, we can't have this ever again. Please don't drink ever again. If you do, we can't continue with you.'

I nodded.

'I even accidentally misheard someone on the phone saying you were dead! I went half an hour believing you were dead, that my first-born son had died before me!'

I told him that he was wrong. Deaths are never declared over the phone. If the death occurs in a hospital the next of kin will be informed face to face. Alternatively, if two police officers knock on your door with their hats off then fear the worst.

Deaths are not declared via phone, fax, e-mail or text. I said this to him and he just shook his head and shrugged his shoulders.

Chapter 13 – Burning the bridges…

Initially I spent most of the time in bed staring at the ceiling like a zombie. I certainly looked the part with half of my head shaved off and criss-crossed by lines of track-like stitches. All I needed to do now was drool at the sides of the mouth or maybe roll back and forth on a rocking chair, and I could look even more convincing. Slowly my strength was starting to build up again and I started walking up and down the ward instead. Occasionally I left the ward for 'a smoke', although I rarely actually smoked the roll-up, and just used it as an excuse to get some fresh air, stare at Whitechapel High Street with its masses of busy people coming and going, and then go back to the ward. A member of staff had given me a baseball cap so that I would not look so 'conspicuous'.

It was an overcast afternoon when I decided to go back to bed. I heard no Russian coming from the cubicle next door. The bed next to me was empty. I stayed in my bed all afternoon with no thoughts and no feelings, like a blank sheet, an empty shell with no religion, no culture, no values, no right and no wrong. I was nothing. This was purity. I would not have to side with anyone or anything anymore. I lobbed my head back onto the pillow and tried to empty my mind even further until a dark-haired middle-aged woman entered the ward. She peered around, looking carefully at the others. As soon as she saw me she gulped. Her dark eyes looked really sad. The woman had her hands placed in front of her with one over the other, as if an 'accused' standing in the dock of a courtroom preparing to enter her plea.

'Hello,' she said, 'do you know who I am?'

I shook my head.

'I'm Sabiha, your mother.'

'Oh,' I nodded.

I told her that I was tired and she smiled and replied that I really looked like it. I cannot remember what she said to me that first day she met me. She had a slight Asian accent which made me wonder if she'd got the wrong person. I don't think she said anything of any real importance; she just sat by my bed silently. Before she left she gave me a hug, during which I promptly winced and became rigid like a statue. As soon as she left I went back to bed, lay down and breathed a sigh of relief.

It was now December and I was eventually discharged to spend time recovering at home. Halima was willing to have me back at the home in east London which the social services were going to pay for. The clingy Asian woman I had just met accompanied me and we went in the cab together.

Out of curiosity I asked her a few questions. I remembered having seen this woman a few times as a three year old. I remembered hearing the word 'custody' and thinking of the thick, creamy, yellow stuff with rhubarb that a Chinese family next door used to feed me.

I remembered toddling around in her presence for an afternoon. She was also with another man whom I did not recognise as my father. They both sat watching pornographic films and drinking heavily. I remembered trying to copy what I was seeing on the screen (a woman who looks like she is screaming whilst a man is hurting her) and trying to imitate the movements. So I asked the Asian woman what this memory was all about.

At first she claimed not to remember but I persisted. Tears then started streaming down her cheek.

She came to visit me every day and would frequently burst into tears at the slightest provocation. If there was anything that she could not reply to she would simply start crying. Suddenly it all made sense. This woman and my father were fighting a custody battle when I was three years old. I had been passed around for the first few years of my life, and the social services had almost taken me away from my father after he once picked me up with a cigarette in his mouth, which accidentally stubbed me on the arm. All this woman would have to do now was to make me behave inappropriately for my age and she would win the case. It was quite logical what she was doing, not very moral some might add, but it made sense. She was trying to get me back by all means possible. She burst into tears again and I yawned repeatedly. Getting the truth from her was difficult so I started working things out for myself. She came across as a woman full of regret and remorse but I was insulted by her frequent apologies. It made me feel that my existence was something to apologise for.

She once phoned me whilst under the influence of alcohol herself; I was bored and wanted to hang up because I had some cans of lager waiting for me in my room. She was crying and slurring that everything was her fault. I told her not to blame herself, that it was not her fault and that I needed to go back to bed.

Deep down I felt sorry for the poor woman who was convinced that she had given birth to an Arab boy called Sheza twenty-three years ago. I started calling her 'mum' just to shut her up.

I was finally twenty-four years of age on the 24th December 2004 and I never thought I would make it this far. The Asian woman and my father always phoned Halima before coming so that they didn't bump into each other. The previous day, my father had come round once again; it was him and my little brother. The boy was growing taller.

Not everyone in a state of drunken blackout immediately throws themselves under trains. Some shout, scream, turn violent; some laugh, joke, turn gregarious; some go home quietly in one piece with nothing significant to recollect. It tells you what kind of person you are when the mind is on autopilot. What struck me was the spontaneity of what I had done. There was no reflection and no thought for the consequences. This was an act of free will.

If not one quick method, maybe there's the 'death by instalments' technique of breaking down suicide into small, manageable, bite-sized chunks: 'one day at a time'. Smoke, drink, eat; simply breathe the air if you can't think of anything else. Maybe live impulsively, engage in 'risky' sexual behaviour, drink-drive. Bleat out the same worn-out cliché of 'live fast, die young'.

Then there's always religion, I suppose. What do you think would have happened to me had Abid actually managed to recruit me? If I actually felt that anything was worth dying for, I'd do it without question. Thank God I'm an atheist.

In the period since then I have paid attention to the comments of others in regards to suicide. Some people will go far enough to dismiss all forms of suicide as 'stupid', 'selfish', 'crazy' or 'cowardly' as if the decision to exist or not does not belong to us. I did not regret what I had done. It was comforting to know that at any point in the future if life gets equally unbearable again I will always have that freedom: the very choice over my own existence.

Eventually I lost my temper with my father. I was fed up with his moral lectures and his appeal to emotions. It was getting boring. Before leaving he told me that if I ever drank again I was to no longer be his son. Halima informed him that I had broken that promise four days later. That bridge had now been burnt.

The house had failed an inspection and I was moved elsewhere. No 'next of kin' had any contact with me now, as I forgot to tell the Asian woman where I was living. I disappeared out of her life as abruptly as she once disappeared out of mine. But this wasn't revenge. I just couldn't be arsed to keep in contact with her. I simply felt nothing. Later on something would happen that would send me back to hospital, and finally I started to figure out why I had transformed into this person I had now become.

Chapter 14 – …the final bridge

The room was bleak and almost bare with the monotony of the walls only broken by nicotine stains and the marks of stubbed out cigarettes. Various overweight people sat around sagging and wilting in all directions whilst crammed into rusty metal chairs. The crucifix-wielding woman opposite me had been in and out of these places for almost twenty years now and been made to frequently sit in confined spaces over long periods of time. She defined herself by the size of the gigantic wooden cross she wore around her neck. It was her cross to bear. She told me that she had bought it from a cheap goods store in Stratford Shopping Centre. The woman told me she had been fed excessive amounts of processed foodstuffs all her life until she developed diabetes mellitus, and was now morbidly obese, could no longer look after herself and spoke like a six-year-old girl trapped in the body of a big, fat, dying fifty year old. She was a consumer. Everyone was defined by what they owned. There was a tobacco aristocracy going on in the room. The majority had rolling tobacco and papers. A few lucky ones had cigarettes. At the bottom were the scroungers and those waiting for the few last drags from someone else's cigarette.

Everyone was sitting around in some great, big death fest of a group in which the sole aim in life was to be cared for by the state. I was back in the psychiatric hospital. Back in the only place I felt I belonged in now.

One woman suddenly came back to life and rushed towards the TV to put the volume up. Her eyes lit up as the box bellowed out the news of London winning the 2012 Olympic bid.

'And I could save the taxpayer a lot of money by killing myself,' I added, 'that could help pay for the…'

'But don't do that!' said the crucifix woman. 'You're worth more than that.'

'I'm a burden on the state,' I replied.

'Jesus loves you,' she said.

'I loved Tower Bridge…' I replied.

'Oh, don't talk about that; Jesus loves you,' she insisted. 'I see visions of Jesus Christ, you know!'

'Yeah, that's why you're here,' I replied.

A few others burst out laughing when I said that. I had suddenly injected some life into the place. It all started with the volume on that telly going up, and then some energy shot out and put life into the others. It all ended when a female nurse came in, told us to put the volume down and all life was put on hold again.

It was for the first time that I had decided to write about any of the things that had happened. I slipped some tatty pages to a female member of staff at the hospital. I wanted to know how long I would be back here. I had the impression that it would be a long time after what I had just done.

I was sat on a late-night bus on my way back to the new "home" that I had been allocated by you lot. A young woman on the bus had black hair and spoke Italian with three others that she was in the company of. The four then struck up a conversation in English with a stranger. They talked comfortably for some time with this stranger.

The stranger then left and then the four of them sat at the back of the bus where I was sitting and carried on talking. The girl looked at me for a split second and I noticed that mournful look again. I caught the same look as she suddenly turned to the others, went back to cheerful and carried on speaking in Italian with them. She left me with a sad look that I could not take away. I spent that night awake in bed staring at the ceiling, unable to get that moment out of my mind. I felt like that look was the embodiment of everything. Unapproachable, not worth the effort, an imposter, undesirable.

I spent the next couple of days in my room. I had been retreating from the world. I quietly got up from the chair. I decided to leave no note and not to tell anyone what I was about to do. I just didn't want to be here anymore. At the station the train came in and I found that I was no longer scared of it. This should be a bad sign but at the time I felt it was a good thing. It was a calm and peaceful journey and I got off at Tower Hill station, got out and turned right. I saw a man with a large badge and clipboard trying to stop passers-by and talk with them. He looked at me and did nothing and I walked past. He'd just confirmed something yet again. I passed an old wall that was maybe Roman or medieval and saw a homeless man sitting by it asking people for spare change. I gave him everything I had in my pocket: any change and the Travelcard.

Grassy hills, trees; I crossed some busy roads. It was a sunny day; I could feel the sun on my face and a slight breeze as I walked up the Bridge past the Tower of London. Along the Bridge I remember blue metal rails on my right and near it was a stone ledge. I dropped my cigarette on the floor and looked at the ledge, jumped onto it and stood there. Below me I could see the water shining from the sunlight.

In the distance along the Bridge I noticed that people were no longer moving. In the corner of my eye it appeared that a crowd had gathered. The whole mass seemed to be getting bigger and they were all watching me. Nobody knew my name, nobody knew who I was, but I was the spectacle to this show. I was not sure if I could back down now. I could make out a small black boat in the distance rapidly heading in my direction. I heard a voice coming from the audience.

"Jump," shouted the voice. It was the voice of a young male and was soon joined by a few other young voices. I felt like I was only there to entertain them.

"Get on with it!" shouted a girl. There was laughter. I decided to jump. I could not back down. I'd be ruining their entertainment.

I had never jumped from such a height before. I tensed up as the wind gushed past and that's why I fell in feet first. As soon as I entered the water I automatically stopped breathing. Everything was muffled and cold. My eyes were open and I could make out the brighter water and the water getting dark. Suddenly it dawned on me that since the impact of landing in the water had not knocked me out I would be fully conscious for the next minute or so. I thought to myself that if I had 60 seconds to live then holding my breath would only prolong this, but I could not get myself to breathe.

Suddenly a jolt hit me. Something had grabbed my leg. As soon as my leg was grabbed an arm enveloped my neck and took me with it. Within a few seconds I was taken up to the surface by someone in a black swimsuit that covered his entire body. I was thrown onto a small black boat with two others on it and immediately a red blanket was placed over my entire body, covering my head entirely. I could hear the black boat speeding off.

I remember little of what happened after this. Maybe unconsciously I do not wish to remember. I really wish I could recollect everything just so that I could know a little of the implications of what I did. I remember that after the boat I was put into a van. In this van my clothes were taken off and I was made to wear a white boiler suit and was taken in an ambulance to a hospital. This is all I remember.

She paused for a moment.

'Thank you for this,' she said.

'It was hard for me to write,' I replied, 'but now I've done it and that I'm aware of what I did how long will I be here?'

'Some time,' she said. 'Although we are grateful for you being honest with us about this, the fact is you could easily have ended up brain-damaged for life had you been in there any longer, so we just can't let you go at present.'

I nodded without argument.

I had calmed down now, and whilst one person had fallen asleep on the sofa and another had his head on the table, I said good-night to anyone else on the ward who still seemed alive but even some of the nurses were nodding off. I went to my room and wrote some things on that piece of paper.

A name, a skin colour and an upbringing does not make you a Muslim. I let my identity be defined by those Muslims, Christians, Jews, Hindus, Buddhists and Sikhs who could not let go of their own identities.

Being a man does not make you a rapist, a predator or a murderer. I let myself be defined by those women who could not let go of their own identities.

Standing on the ledge does not mean that for that very moment I have to adopt the label of "suicidal young man". I did not have to mould my identity to suit the spectator. I had the choice of stepping back.

I was not observing the look on the girl's face. I was observing the effect that her look was having on me. She wasn't some symbol of how all women have ever seen me. I was wrong.

It reminded me of the case I once heard about a Polish farmer who had supposedly committed suicide because he lost his mobile phone. Nobody can really understand why anyone would do something as major as kill oneself over such a petty reason, unless they've considered the symbolism of it all. Now I could understand how the man would have felt, the changes that had taken place in his life, the developments in technology, human relations, values that were taking place in Poland since the collapse of communism. This could all have led the man to feel he was watching by helplessly while the world moved on. The farmer did not commit suicide over a phone. He decided life was no longer worth living once a symbol of *communication* with others had 'abandoned' him. It was the last straw in a catalogue of incidents that he must have felt had undermined him and rendered him undesirable.

Albert Camus was right; the worm really is in the man's heart. Sartre was right; hell really is other people. Not because the tube in summer is hot, or commuters around you can be annoying, but because our actions, beliefs and ways of behaving are done with other people's judgements of us in mind. I was so scared of rejection that I'd find my own way out first. That's what I had done with the red-haired girl right at the beginning.

I decided to write three more words on the paper:

I am nothing.

I never had to be the victim of anything. I never had to be the perpetrator of anything. Now I was free.

The next day, fifty-three people perished on the London Underground in a series of orchestrated attacks. As everything unravelled afterwards, people's identities started coming out: not just the victims, not just the bombers, but those of everyone around. Some of the Muslim patients feared a backlash or were in strong denial blaming the MI5 or the CIA. Some of the non-Muslims actually talked of 'fighting back'. Others sat in the smoking room talking to themselves. I heard sentences beginning with 'we Muslims…', 'we English…', 'we…', 'they…', 'them…', 'us…'. Everyone on the ward immediately formed an 'identity'. Sometimes the 'I' and the 'we' converged and the lines became blurred. The ones with a personality disorder were the ones with the greatest identity confusion. Most had no identity, so they latched onto the identities of others.

I remembered a slogan I had once heard: 'All men are potential rapists'.

Initially this scared me because I am supposed to be a 'man' but I have no desire to commit rape. Merely having a pair of hands makes you a potential murderer. But I now understood that what this slogan set out to do was the feminist version of the ideology of victimisation. By identifying men as the 'perpetrator' and women as the 'victims' then being a victim becomes a core part of one's identity as a woman. An inferiority complex sets in and everything done in life is based around the role as the oppressed. For as long as this remains the case one can be no other than a victim – It has become a self-imposed label, a raison d'etre, the role in life. Instead of promoting individual strength there is now collective weakness. The lowest common denominator becomes the bounds that tie us together, whether it be race, gender, sexuality, religion or disability. I suddenly decided that I wasn't mentally ill at all.

I then thought of Abid again. I wondered what I would have been like had his particular group of Muslims, with their own particular interpretation and way of seeing the world, actually won me over. They would all talk about persecution of Muslims. They would talk of Palestine, Afghanistan, Iraq, Chechnya, Bosnia, but would never talk of Muslim society persecuting both fellow Muslims and non-Muslims alike. It would not fit in with the role of 'victim' if they did. If they did they would justify it as 'self-defence' and 'fighting back'. Middle England also has a persecution complex; there are supposedly gypsies under the bed, asylum seekers behind the fridge, gays and lesbians in the closet and taxmen at the door. The white working class feel victimised too; as if everyone else gets homes and housing except for them. Suddenly a besieged mentality sets in and we're all victims pointing the finger at one another; assault becomes self-defence, revenge becomes justice, and murder becomes martyrdom.

I am not saying that none of us are the victims of anything; I'm saying that we are ALL the victims of something. I had been a *'victim'* for too long; women could see that when they looked at me. Maria saw that; Sabiha felt that, all the women I had met along the way could sense it. They could see it in my posture, my facial expression, body language and even my rate of breathing. It had become my identity, the only secure identity I felt I had in life and an identity that I had been willing to pursue to the point of death. I wanted to go back into the outside world and start again. This time I was to make the change from 'self' to 'Self'. It was time to let go and be free.

Chapter 15 – Neither victim nor criminal

It was the year 2006; I was now a 25 year old, had just finally come out of hospital and was now living back at a hostel. I stood outside Whitechapel station smoking a cigarette before catching a tube. It was a bitter, late afternoon in January and the sky was getting darker. Running around were young children on their way to Mosque, accompanied by their mothers, many of whom dressed head to toe in full-length *niqaab* like the two black phantoms that once hid away from me at the flat on Commercial Street.

I chucked my cigarette butt on the floor and just before I turned round to enter the station I took one last look at that large, grey stone building opposite me across the street. It was the hospital that I had been brought to countless times: usually by ambulance, occasionally by police van and once by helicopter. I peered to my side and noticed that a young woman of Asian appearance had been observing me from a few metres away. She had beautiful dark eyes with thick kohl around them, giving her the appearance of a Cleopatra.

'Hi there,' she smiled, 'are you in a hurry or do you have to go anywhere?'

I was on my way to attend a group meeting elsewhere in London but that could wait.

'Er…no.'

'Where are you from?' she asked.

I paused for a second.

'Here,' I replied.

'I mean which country?'

I shrugged my shoulders and said 'Egypt'. She then came closer.

'Are you looking for business?'

I looked at her calmly.

'No,' I replied, 'it's OK.'

'There's no rush,' she added.

'No, sorry.'

'Why not, though?' she asked.

I gently told her that I had never had sex before and that I did not want my first time to be this way. She said that there was 'no rush' and I agreed that I was in no rush to have sex. She looked at me incredulously and told me that that was not what she meant. She carried on asking me if I just wanted a blow job or a hand job. I suddenly noticed her hands. They were small, feminine, Bollywood hands but a careful look revealed they were rough and coarse; my own were soft and smooth by comparison.

'No,' I gently nodded.

She then asked me for a cigarette to which I duly obliged. I also handed her a few pound coins from my pocket. I knew that any money she got she would spend on drugs but I did not care because that is what I would do.

She went on her way and I quickly finished off my second cigarette that I had lit up without even thinking. As I entered the station I gave her one last look mournfully and smiled.

'No matter what guys may think of you. No matter what other girls may think of you. After the arrests, sectionings, banning and fights people look down on me too. Fuck 'em – I'm with you on this, not them.'

There was something not genuine about this thought I had. I was not to realise what it was until much later on in the day.

I suddenly felt a sick feeling in my stomach as the buckling sound of the tracks indicated that the train was coming. Suddenly the image of a train charging in on my left with me falling in front of it flashed into my mind. The image suddenly left me as quickly as it had appeared and I decided to stand well away from the platform edge as possible before getting in the train once the doors opened. If I was now feeling scared of the train, I thought then, this must be a good sign.

It was now evening and I was sitting in a dingy church basement in north London sipping coffee from a polystyrene cup. It was a meeting with a cult-like organisation that was set up in Ohio in America in 1935, called *Alcoholics Anonymous*. The beginning of the meeting consisted of ritualistic readings of a preamble and part of a chapter from a 'Big Book'. A man then asked if there were any newcomers who had been sober for less than thirty days and would like to introduce themselves, adding that 'this is not to embarrass you but to simply give you the warm welcome we have all once received'. I put my hand up and told them that my name is Sheza and that I am an alcoholic. Suddenly thirty or so people said 'Hello, Sheza' in unison. I told them that this was my first meeting. The truth was that I had been drifting from meeting to meeting across London for almost six months. I noticed that a speaker at each meeting would always go through the same routine whilst talking. The first routine would be to describe how they always felt that they were 'different' since they were always unlike others throughout their childhoods. The next would be to dive into a lurid story of drinking episodes, failed relationships, job loses, hospitalisations and, in the case of this particular speaker, long periods spent in prison. Next would be to describe how they desperately turned to Alcoholics Anonymous despite all the 'God talk', how they worked through 'twelve steps', 'got a sponsor' and found God, or a 'higher power', as they call it. The speaker would then talk about how his life had been transformed, how he owes his life to AA and how grateful he was to be here. After he finally shut up everyone started clapping. Others would then thank the speaker for the chair and boast about similar incidents for a period of three minutes. I noticed a sense of fear in a few of the members. Roughly a third of the group looked indignant and remained silent. One woman did talk, eventually broke down and revealed how she was 'fucking fed up with the whole steps this, steps that, God this, God that' issue. She was soon interrupted and agreed to stop talking. She took a tissue out of her handbag and wiped her eyes. At the end of the meeting we all had to stand in a circle holding hands and recite the following words:

God grant me the serenity,
to accept the things I cannot change,
courage to change the things I can,
and the wisdom to know the difference.

Keep coming back! You're worth it! You're worth it! You're worth it!!

After the meeting a few male members of the group clustered around me, shook my hand and asked me if I 'had a sponsor'. I said that I did not. One man replied that it was essential that I get this sponsor, a member of AA who has been part of the organisation longer than me, to individually help me and take me 'through the steps'. Another man said it was 'essential' and that there was 'no other way to achieve sobriety'.

'No other way?' I asked.

'No other way,' he insisted adamantly.

'I don't believe in God,' I replied. 'How am I going to go through these steps?'

Suddenly one man's eyes lit up:

'But you don't have to believe in some bearded man in the clouds! Your higher power can be anything you want.'

'The fact is,' replied another, 'alcohol has become a power greater than yourself! So you need a power greater than yourself to defeat it! Do you really want to stop drinking, Sheza?'

I said I'd like to but I did not know if I could.

'So why are you in an AA meeting?' asked another.

I looked towards the door where I could see a group of females. Some of the other females were surrounding a female newcomer and smiling, asking her questions and giving her their numbers. I wondered who that young woman was. I wished I could have just approached her but I would not have known what to say. She suddenly looked at me and I smiled instead of looking away. A part of me felt just the imposter here, as I once was in the Soho church with the blonde German. I knew why I was here.

I noticed that the men were still waiting for an answer from me.

'I'm here because I want to keep sober,' I replied, knowing that if I kept coming back to this meeting I would have an excuse to talk to that girl.

'Are you willing to go to any lengths to do it?' he promptly asked me.

I nodded my head.

'Here, have my mobile number,' he continued. 'You need to attend some more meetings. I bet slowly you'll start to identify.'

That last word struck me like a club: identify, identity, identification.

By the end of that meeting I had the phone numbers of a dozen male AA members. I looked one more time at the fellow newcomer girl as she walked off into the distance, and my heart sank.

I decided I would keep coming back but only because of *her*. Nothing had changed.

After the meeting I decided to return to Whitechapel High Street to drink the evening away with my head down. The pub was exactly opposite the largest Mosque in east London where some men had once prayed for an atheist who attempted suicide. As I sat in there I peered towards the window. There the word was in green Arabic letters across the street: my past, my judgement, my authority, my wrath, my bondage, my father figure. I suddenly turned my back. I was free now but I did not like this self-imposed isolation. I then realised how fragile this freedom was. I had turned 'recovering alcoholic' into my new-found identity, but here I was sitting in a pub clutching a pint in my hand. My new identity was over in minutes. I wondered what the point in being free was if I knew nothing of what I was in the first place. Those in AA realised this so they do what many others do; they bury themselves into a large organisation, submit themselves to a higher power and mould themselves into whatever is expected of them. They feel free because they do not have to think for themselves; they will do what their 'sponsor' suggests, do what the 'twelve steps' suggest, and do what the 'Big Book' of Alcoholics Anonymous suggests they do.

Now I knew why I was so scared at Whitechapel station when the train approached. I was aware that I was having flashbacks. Nothing was stopping me from doing what I once did again except for my own identity as a human being who wishes to keep living, but if I was so sure of this identity, of this 'will to live', I wondered then why I was so scared of jumping again. My identity was never secure; I was neither perpetrator nor victim.

As I approached Whitechapel station again and finished off the cigarette, this time three young Asian men approached. I suddenly straightened up for the inevitable demands for a cigarette, money or of what I was 'looking at'. The memories of north London immediately came back, which inevitably led to Maria. It suddenly struck me as unimportant in light of what may actually happen to me within the next few minutes.

'Bro, where are you from?' one of them asked.

'Here,' I replied.

'No, I mean *originally*.'

I said 'Iran'.

The man next to him then replied:

'You were talking to that girl earlier?'

I asked him to explain and I nodded when his description of the prostitute was spot on.

'Listen,' he added, 'don't fall for anything she says. She hangs out with these guys by the bus stops. If she says anything and you agree, and you and she go off together into a back lane…her guys will be waiting. They'll pull out a knife and take everything off you. She'll simply stand back and keep a look out.'

I nodded and said thanks for the warning.

I managed to get that train and on the carriage I sat back, closed my eyes and took a deep breath. I reviewed what I had thought earlier:

'No matter what guys may think of you. No matter what other girls may think of you. After the arrests, sectionings, banning and fights people look down on me too. Fuck 'em – I'm with you on this, not them.'

I smiled when I realised how wrong I was. I was judging with the 'us and them' mentality. I was trying to identify with her and I was identifying us both as the *victims*, just like what Maria had done with me and just like the Asian woman who said she was my mother. I was dressing the prostitute up in the clothes I wanted her to wear. I was turning her into the kind of person I wanted her to be, that I wished her to be, that I felt she should be.

It did not matter what her intentions were. I was simply a male she knew for a few minutes and she wanted her next fix. Why should I have thought that in her eyes I would be different to any other man who she knew? Was it because I considered myself a *victim* too? If I went ahead with it I would have been mugged of everything at knifepoint (including some of the rough notes for the outline of what you are reading right now). So I would have been the victim of armed robbery? True. I would also have been the victim of my own moralising, and if I were to carry on like that I would take out my self-righteousness and 'self-defence' on others. The cycle would never stop. I would always consider myself a victim.

Yet again I told myself to stop labelling myself anything. Not having to be treated 'differently' because I've 'seen things' that others have or have not. Not to patronise others with 'I've been there too', or to use my past to manipulate others, feed on their guilt complexes and milk their sense of sympathy; never to have to label myself a survivor, victim, perpetrator, and to never have to be permanently 'in recovery' – because the one thing you'll never recover from is your own recovery.

As I had done some years ago, I took another look at the passengers around me. I immediately noticed an old man who was standing up so I decided to give up my seat. He said 'Thank you'. I then looked at everyone else. Everyone was still miserable, only a bit more tired looking. Now I had found out what was truly going on. Albert Camus once remarked that the only real problem in philosophy was that of suicide. I once found it strange that contemplating the voluntary taking of my own life could be the start of a new way of seeing the world. I had been searching for meaning; I was searching for an identity but I would never get it here. I thought for a moment as the train rolled its way into Mile End station. Nobody said a word. Despite the din of the train and the tannoy, there was a familiar silence, an indifference of the world that I had always been disturbed by. I now knew why I was scared of freedom. From now on I had a choice; I could either search for an ultimate meaning in life, and never find it, or give up and end it all.

I can choose to carry on living; I can say that my life is absurd, that it has no meaning and that it is pointless, but that does not have to entail suicide.

I no longer gave a damn about God, about culture, about Islam or Christianity. I no longer had to feel lucky or unlucky to be alive, grateful or ungrateful, desirable or undesirable. It did not matter. I did not see the point in joining any rat race or climbing my way up any social ladder. From now on I would be happy with my futile attempts to understand a universe that goes beyond my limited consciousness; this is philosophy. My new salvation. Knowing that there is so much I shall never know.

Something then suddenly struck my attention – I was the only person on that Underground carriage who was smiling.

Lightning Source UK Ltd.
Milton Keynes UK
30 November 2010

163672UK00001B/72/P

9 781849 913294